the
Standard
CUT GLASS
Value Guide

1981-1982 Price Update

by Jo Evers

COLLECTOR BOOKS
P. O. BOX 3009
PADUCAH, KENTUCKY 42001

The current values in this book should be used only as a guide. They are not intended to set prices, which vary from one section of the country to another. Auction prices as well as dealer prices vary greatly and are affected by condition as well as demand. Neither the Author nor the Publisher assumes responsibility for any losses that might be incurred as a result of consulting this guide.

Additional copies of this book may be ordered from:

COLLECTOR BOOKS
P.O. Box 3009
Paducah, Kentucky 42001

@$8.95 Add $1.00 for postage and handling.

Copyright: Bill Schroeder, 1981
ISBN: 0-89145-002-5
Values Updated for 1981

Printed by IMAGE GRAPHICS, Paducah, Kentucky

The Cut Glass Industry in America

Though cut glass did not appear in mass in the United States before the early 1800's, its true origin goes back to ancient times. The Egyptians before the time of Christ made and cut glass as did craftsmen in ancient Rome. And, even though there have been many refinements and a constant evolution in the process of creating cut glass, it remains a process of grinding decorations into glassware by means of a metal or stone cutting tool.

European life and craftsmanship greatly influenced the life of Americans during the early years of this country. In the same way, the cut glass styles and designs of Europe were a heavy influence on the glass made in America. The early designs were generally simple fluting, diamonds and similar patterns. By the late 1800's, however, American cut glass design had come of age with more complex patterns and series of designs. Cut glass craftsmanship in this country had a struggle for recognition despite the quality of the glass being produced here. In the beginning, glass sellers refused to recognize domestic glass and advertised it as European imports. The major glass producers waged a campaign to promote the excellent quality of American cut glass. Still, it wasn't until the Centennial Exposition in 1876 and finally the World's Columbian Exposition in 1893 that the American public really began to accept American manufactured cut glass as products of true quality.

Boston and New York became prime centers of cut glass production and several glass houses began operation in these cities. The industry grew and gradually spread through the New England states, the midwest and finally even the west coast.

Many important advancements and improvements came into the production of cut glass. Probably the most important step was the move to an assembly line type of production. Before this had been tried, a glass cutter would work from start to finish on one piece of glassware. With the assembly line, several workers could be assigned a specific task in the cutting process, making the work flow smoother and faster. In addition, a worker could become more skilled in a certain process as he practiced it only, and the glassware would benefit from a better quality overall.

Mechanized cutting was another important advancement to the cut glass industry. It was widely used and accepted in the European countries, but the American industry never really accepted the use of a machine for cutting glass. The American glass makers generally felt that the craftsman was needed to produce true quality cut glass.

One advancement to the cut glass industry lead to a degrading of the product and is responsible for so many "look alike" near cut and pressed glass products. This new step was the use of pressed blanks for cutting. Although it was a mechanized process and allowed more people to afford cut glass, it eventually lead to the widespread manufacture and sale of pressed glass.

Making a piece of cut crystal is a process that involves many small steps. First the blanks, or original glass item, must be made. The raw materials are melted down and poured into a mold where they cooled into a "blank". When cooled, these molded blanks must have some type of notation as to the pattern required for cutting. This is done by marking the pattern to be cut directly on the glass. The actual cutting is done with a stone or metal wheel that is dripped with some type of abrasive agent and pressed against the surface to be cut. A cutter would always work from the deepest etchings to the most shallow, since the deep cuts produced the most strain on the glass and a break at the beginning proved to be less of a loss in materials and man hours.

The cuts made into the glass originally have a dull grey appearance and must be polished to give the item a unified look. The polishing is done on a wood wheel that has had rouge or another type of polishing solution applied to it. As production of cut glass became more mechanized, the polishing wheel was gradually replaced by a solution of acid in which the piece of cut glass was dipped for polishing.

Signing a piece of cut glass also involves the use of an acid solution. A pre-cut die with the company emblem or trademark was saturated with acid and pressed into the desired location on the glass.

More shallow cuts or engravings appear on many pieces of crystal. The engraved design is marked on the blank in much the same way the design to be cut is marked. For the process of engraving, a wheel is still used, this time a revolving copper one. The wheel etches the design which is usually left in matte to compliment the deeper shiney cut edges on the glass. In some cases, however, the shallow engraved surfaces were preferred and allowed to stand alone.

Many times it is difficult to differentiate between cut and pressed glass. Cut glass will generally have a slight "ring" to it when thumped, due to the large lead content. This lead content also gives cut glass a heavy feel. Another method of determining cut from pressed glass is by studying the indentations. Cut glass will generally have sharp, crisp edges while pressed glass tends to have rounded, less perfect edges. Light will also refract in the cut edges and indentations and not in pressed edges.

PRICING

The prices in this catalog are for near perfect to perfect pieces of cut crystal. It is, of course, extremely difficult to find a piece of mint-perfect cut glass today. Small, minute rim and edge chips can be found on most any piece. Cracked or badly damaged pieces of cut glass are, for all practical purposes, worthless on today's market. Look for cracks in deep cut seams in good light, carefully turning at different angles to expose the flaw. Edge and rim chips can be felt as well as seen by the experienced cut glass collector. Finding flaws in cut glass is probably more difficult than in any other type of glass because of the many cuts, edges and facets. ''Let the buyer beware.'' The prices in this book are to be used only as a guide. We have used recent sales catalogs, auction reports, show prices and dealer values to arrive at a retail value.

BASKETS, HANDLED

Pitkins & Brooks
PANSY BASKET,
ENGRAVED
P & B Grade
8'' 318.00-348.00

Pitkins & Brooks
DAISY HANDLED
BASKET, ENGRAVED
P & B Grade
8'' 320.00-345.00

Pitkins & Brooks
ELDORADO HANDLED
BASKET
Standard Grade
8'' 276.00-300.00

Pitkins & Brooks
SUNBEAM HANDLED
BASKET
P & B Grade
7½'' 244.00-281.00

Pitkins & Brooks
ELDORADO HANDLED
BASKET
Standard Grade
6'' 162.00-222.00
8'' 234.00-282.00

Pitkins & Brooks
OSBORNE HANDLED
BASKET
P & B Grade
6'' 217.50-285.50

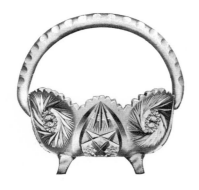

Pitkins & Brooks
ZESTA BASKET
P & B Grade
8'' handled
& footed . . .275.00-300.00

Pitkins & Brooks
ZESTA HANDLED
BASKET
P & B Grade
7'' 278.00-297.00

BELLS

T. B. Clark & Co.
BELLS, JEWEL
Lge. size . . . 136.00-142.00
Sm. size . . . 118.00-124.00

Pitkins & Brooks
DEAN CALL BELL
P & B Grade
5½" 135.00-141.00

CALL BELL
5½" 136.00-142.00

TEA BELL
5½" 125.50-143.50

TEA BELL
5¾" 139.00-145.00

J. D. Bergen
PREMIER
6" bell 141.00-153.00
7" bell 159.00-171.00

CALL BELL
Buzz Star Cutting
Each 134.00-152.00

BON-BONS

J. D. Bergen
EMBLEM
Olive or
Bon Bon 37.50-47.50

J. D. Bergen
EVELYN
6'' Olive or
Bon Bon 48.50-64.50

J. D. Bergen
BEDFORD
7'' Olive
or Bon Bon . . 49.50-59.50

Pitkins & Brooks
HALLE BON BON
P & B Grade
6'' 50.50-55.50

Pitkins & Brooks
BEVERLY
P & B Grade
6'' 89.50-114.50

Pitkins & Brooks
ORIOLE
Standard Grade
6'' 41.50-51.50

Pitkins & Brooks
RAJAH BON BON
P & B Grade
6¾'' 71.50-95.50
Standard Grade
6¾'' 47.50-65.50

Pitkins & Brooks
MYRTLE BON BON
Standard Grade
7½'' 34.00-40.00

Pitkins & Brooks
MARS BON BON
P & B Grade
3½'' 48.00-60.00
Standard Grade
3½'' 30.00-36.00

Pitkins & Brooks
RAJAH BON BON
P & B Grade
7¼'' 79.00-96.00

Higgins & Seiter
WEBSTER
Salted Almond Dish
6'' 36.00-51.00

Higgins & Seiter
WALTER SCOTT
Olive or Bon Bon,
Heart Shape
5'' 35.00-52.00

T. B. Clark & Co.
ARBUTUS
Bon Bon
Each 64.00-79.00

BON-BONS

J. D. Bergen
DARIEL
Olive or Bon Bon
5''x9''......90.50-101.50

J. D. Bergen
MAGNET
Olive or Bon Bon
8''.........77.00-88.00

J. D. Bergen
THELMA
Olive or Bon Bon
9''.........79.00-89.00

J. D. Bergen
HAWTHORNE
Olive or Bon Bon
5''x9''.......76.00-86.00

J. D. Bergen
LAUREL
Olive or Bon Bon
7''.........56.00-71.00

Pitkins & Brooks
DELMAR COVERED
BON BON
P & B Grade
10''.......365.00-415.00

J. D. Bergen
ARGO
Olive or Bon Bon
7''.........70.00-80.00

Averbeck
DIAMOND
Each.......82.50-105.50

Pitkins & Brooks
GARLAND COVERED
BON BON
4''..............45.00-55.00
5''..............50.00-60.00
6''..............55.00-70.00

BON-BONS

T. B. Clark & Co.
MANHATTAN
Bon Bon
Each 48.00-58.00

T. B. Clark & Co.
MANHATTAN
Bon Bon
Each 44.00-55.00

T. B. Clark & Co.
ST. GEORGE
Each 58.00-63.00

Higgins & Seiter
WALTER SCOTT
Olive or Bon Bon
5½'' 30.00-36.00

T. B. Clark & Co.
BON BON, JEWEL
Each 31.00-37.00

T. B. Clark & Co.
BON BON, ADONIS
Each 125.00-131.00

T. B. Clark & Co.
BON BON, ST. GEORGE
Each 58.00-63.00

Higgins & Seiter
NAPOLEON
Ice Cream, Olive or
Bon Bon
6'' 35.00-46.00

Higgins & Seiter
WALTER SCOTT
Olive or Bon Bon
6'' 44.00-55.00

T. B. Clark & Co.
DORRANCE
Bon Bon
Each 60.00-77.00

T. B. Clark & Co.
WINOLA
Bon Bon
Each 58.00-69.00

Higgins & Seiter
ARLINGTON
Handled Bon Bon
6'' 42.00-48.00

Higgins & Seiter
ARLINGTON
Saucer or Bon Bon
5'' 40.00-46.00
6'' 57.00-68.00

Higgins & Seiter
WALTER SCOTT
Oblong Olive, Pickle
or Bon Bon
4''x7'' 52.00-63.00

T. B. Clark & Co.
BON BON, JEWEL
Each 41.00-52.00

T. B. Clark & Co.
ST. GEORGE
Rd. Handled Bon Bon
5'' 46.00-57.00
6'' 63.00-79.00

T. B. Clark & Co.
IRVING
Handled Bon Bon
5'' 47.00-57.00
6'' 63.00-80.00

T. B. Clark & Co.
JEFFERSON
Handled Bon Bon
5'' 55.00-65.00
6'' 70.00-85.00

BON-BONS

Pitkins & Brooks
EARL BON BON
P & B Grade
5½" 62.00-67.00
Standard Grade
5½" 42.00-52.00

Averbeck
LADY CURZON
Each 47.00-57.00

Averbeck
PUCK
Each 47.00-57.00

Pitkins & Brooks
NELLORE BON BON
Standard Grade
5½" 34.50-44.50

Pitkins & Brooks
MARS BON BON
P & B Grade
6¾" 77.00-92.00

Averbeck
SARATOGA
Each 47.00-57.00

Averbeck
AMERICAN BEAUTY
5" 72.00-77.00
6" 82.00-92.00

Averbeck
RUBY
5" 37.00-47.00
6" 52.00-57.00

Pitkins & Brooks
ERMINIE BON BON
P & B Grade
6" 34.50-39.50
Standard Grade
6" 24.50-39.50

Pitkins & Brooks
PLYMOUTH
BON BON
P & B Grade
Each 94.50-104.50

Pitkins & Brooks
STEUBEN BON BON
P & B Grade
5¼" 27.00-38.00
Standard Grade
5¼" 14.00-20.00

Pitkins & Brooks
ERIC BON BON
P & B Grade
6" 52.00-67.00
Standard Grade
6" 47.00-52.00

Averbeck
RUBY
Each 37.00-47.00

Higgins & Seiter
WALTER SCOTT
Oblong Olive, Pickle
or Bon Bon
4"x8" 30.00-40.00

Higgins & Seiter
WALTER SCOTT
Olive or Bon Bon
Each 37.00-47.00

BON-BONS

J. D. Bergen
KEY WEST
Olive or Bon Bon
6'' 52.00-67.00

Pitkins & Brooks
HIAWATHA BOAT
BON BON
P & B Grade
9'' 87.00-112.00

Averbeck
NICE
Each 74.50-94.50

Pitkins & Brooks
OAK LEAF
BON BON
P & B Grade
5½'' 52.00-62.00

Averbeck
PARIS
Each 47.00-57.00

Pitkins & Brooks
PRINCE
P & B Grade
6'' 47.00-57.00

Pitkins & Brooks
OSBORNE BON BON
P & B Grade
7'' 57.00-77.00

Averbeck
DIAMOND
Each 57.00-82.00

Averbeck
AMERICAN BEAUTY
5'' 52.00-67.00
6'' 62.00-77.00

Pitkins & Brooks
ESTHER BON BON
Standard Grade
3¼'' 47.00-57.00

Averbeck
NAPLES
Each 69.50-84.50

Averbeck
MARIETTA
Each 52.00-62.00

Pitkins & Brooks
CRESCENT BON BON
P & B Grade
4¾'' 42.00-52.00

Pitkins & Brooks
MYRTLE BON BON
P & B Grade
4¾'' 47.00-57.00

Pitkins & Brooks
PINTO BON BON
P & B Grade
6'' 72.00-82.00
7'' 87.00-97.00

BON-BONS

J. D. Bergen
RIPPLE
Olive or Bon Bon
6" 62.00-77.00

Averbeck
FLEUR DE LIS
Each 44.50-59.50

J. D. Bergen
BRIGHTON
Olive or Bon Bon
7" 34.50-49.50

Averbeck
PUCK
Each 47.00-57.00

Averbeck
DIAMOND
Each 52.00-67.00

Averbeck
RUBY
5" 42.00-57.00
6" 52.00-62.00

Averbeck
SARATOGA
Each 37.00-42.00

Averbeck
AMERICAN BEAUTY
Each 49.50-59.50

Averbeck
AMERICAN BEAUTY
5" 52.00-72.00
6" 57.00-87.00

Pitkins & Brooks
PIZO BON BON
P & B Grade
7" 92.00-97.00

Pitkins & Brooks
HEART BON BON
P & B Grade
5½" 52.00-57.00
Standard Grade
5½" 62.00-77.00

J. D. Bergen
PILGRIM
Bon Bon
6" 59.50-69.50

J. D. Bergen
DIADEM
Bon Bon or Spoon Tray
8" 82.00-92.00

J. D. Bergen
EMBLEM
Olive or Bon Bon
Each 49.50-59.50

BON-BONS

J. D. Bergen
MAGNET
Olive or Bon Bon
6½'' 44.50-54.50

Pitkins & Brooks
RAJAH BON BON
P & B Grade
7½'' 49.00-77.00

J. D. Bergen
JUNO
Olive or Bon Bon
7'' 57.00-67.00

J. D. Bergen
RUTH
Olive or Bon Bon
4''x6½'' 49.00-64.00
5''x7'' 59.00-80.00

T. B. Clark & Co.
BON BON, JEWEL
Each 34.50-49.50

J. D. Bergen
MADISON
Bon Bon or Spoon Tray
8'' 42.00-52.00

J. D. Bergen
CAPRICE
Olive or Bon Bon
7'' 42.00-52.00

Pitkins & Brooks
MEADVILLE
Bon Bon
Standard Grade
7'' 47.00-57.00

J. D. Bergen
MAGNET
Olive or Bon Bon
7½'' 57.00-77.00

J. D. Bergen
KEYSTONE
Olive or Bon Bon
7'' 62.00-77.00

Pitkins & Brooks
MEADVILLE
Bon Bon
Standard Grade
6½'' 32.00-42.00

J. D. Bergen
LAUREL
Olive or Bon Bon
7'' 42.00-57.00

BOWLS

Higgins & Seiter
FLORIDA
Fruit or Berry Bowl
9¼"x13½" . 82.00-107.00

T. B. Clark & Co.
MANHATTAN
Priscilla Bowls
8" 145.00-165.00
9" 180.00-205.00

Higgins & Seiter
TORNADO
Nappie, Low Fruit,
Salad or Berry Bowl
8" 79.00-96.00
9" 101.00-123.00
10" 107.00-134.00

Higgins & Seiter
MONARCH
Cut Glass Bowl
8" 121.50-126.50
9" 127.50-143.50
10" 159.50-176.50

Higgins & Seiter
JUBILEE
Rich Cut Glass Bowl
8" 115.00-143.00
9" 143.00-170.00
10" 159.00-198.00

Higgins & Seiter
WEBSTER
Nut, Fruit or Berry Bowl
8" 97.00-113.00
9" 106.00-113.00
10" 146.00-168.00

T. B. Clark & Co.
ARBUTUS
7" 93.50-104.50
8" 126.50-137.50
9" 143.50-170.50
10" 159.50-181.50

Pitkins & Brooks
MARS FANCY BOWL
P & B Grade
9½" 121.50-148.50

T. B. Clark & Co.
DESDEMONA
8" 107.50-127.50
9" 132.50-157.50
10" 157.50-182.50
12" 187.50-217.50

Pitkins & Brooks
VENICE SALAD BOWL
P & B Grade
8" 77.00-82.00
9" 99.00-109.00

Pitkins & Brooks
MYRTLE SALAD BOWL
Standard Grade
8" 47.00-69.00

Pitkins & Brooks
**MEADVILLE SALAD
BOWL**
Standard Grade
8" 49.50-60.50
9" 71.50-82.50

BOWLS

T. B. Clark & Co.
PRISCILLA - ORIENT
7'' 162.50-182.50
8'' 192.50-227.50
9'' 252.50-312.50

T. B. Clark & Co.
MANHATTAN
7'' 71.50-82.50
8'' 82.50-99.50
9'' 99.50-115.50
10'' 126.50-143.50

T. B. Clark & Co.
VENUS
8'' 155.00-165.00
9'' 180.00-195.00
10'' 215.00-225.00

T. B. Clark & Co.
ADONIS
9'' 235.00-255.00

T. B. Clark & Co.
WINOLA
7'' 66.00-77.00
8'' 82.00-99.00
9'' 99.00-126.00

T. B. Clark & Co.
DESDEMONA
9'' 160.00-185.00

Higgins & Seiter
8'' 66.50-77.50
9'' 82.50-93.50
10'' 104.50-115.50

Higgins & Seiter
GLEN
Nappie or Berry Bowl
8'' 79.00-91.00
9'' 96.00-124.00
10'' 124.00-140.00

T. B. Clark & Co.
ADONIS
7'' 130.00-145.00
8'' 145.00-170.00
9'' 170.00-185.00
10'' 190.00-225.00

Higgins & Seiter
ARLINGTON
8'' 46.00-63.00
9'' 63.00-68.00
10'' 85.00-104.00

T. B. Clark & Co.
VENUS
8'' 127.50-147.50
9'' 147.50-157.50
10'' 167.50-187.50
12'' 217.50-237.50

T. B. Clark & Co.
ARBUTUS
8'' 105.00-130.00
9'' 165.00-180.00
10'' 185.00-200.00

BOWLS

Pitkins & Brooks
MIKADO SALAD BOWL
P & B Grade
8" 63.00-74.00

Pitkins & Brooks
DUCHESS SALAD BOWL
P & B Grade
8" 190.00-210.00

Pitkins & Brooks
CARNEGIE SALAD
BOWL
P & B Grade
8" 99.00-121.00

Pitkins & Brooks
RAJAH FANCY BOWL
P & B Grade
8" 155.00-190.00

Pitkins & Brooks
NELLORE SALAD
BOWL
P & B Grade
8" 68.00-80.00

Pitkins & Brooks
LYRE SALAD BOWL
Standard Grade
8" 38.50-44.50

Pitkins & Brooks
ORIOLE FANCY
BOWL - OVAL
P & B Grade
10" 82.50-99.50

Averbeck
ACME BOWL
7" 70.50-80.50
8" 87.50-97.50
9" 97.50-112.50
10" 112.50-127.50

Pitkins & Brooks
VENICE SALAD BOWL
P & B Grade
8" 82.50-93.50
9" 93.50-110.50

Averbeck
OCCIDENT BOWL
7" 105.00-125.00
8" 125.00-145.00
9" 145.00-175.00
10" 170.00-210.00

Averbeck
WEBSTER
Fruit, Salad or Berry
8" 69.00-80.00
9" 85.00-102.00
10" 96.00-89.00

Higgins & Seiter
MONARCH
Nappie
8" 80.00-91.00
9" 96.00-112.00
10" 112.00-140.00

BOWLS

T. B. Clark & Co.
MANHATTAN
7" 64.00-82.00
8" 82.00-94.00
9" 106.00-124.00
10" 124.00-184.00
12" 154.00-214.00

Higgins & Seiter
8" 48.00-60.00
9" 66.00-78.00
10" 84.00-96.00

T. B. Clark & Co.
CARNATION
8" 142.50-172.50
9" 172.50-202.50
10" 252.50-277.50

Higgins & Seiter
TORNADO
8" 84.00-102.00
9" 108.00-114.00

Higgins & Seiter
CORONET
8" 57.00-63.00

Higgins & Seiter
PEERLESS
Salad, Fruit or
Berry Bowl with Tray
Each 150.00-190.00

T. B. Clark & Co.
DESDEMONA
Each 185.00-225.00

T. B. Clark & Co.
PALMETTO
9" 174.00-210.00

T. B. Clark & Co.
ADONIS
Each 220.00-250.00

Higgins & Seiter
LISBON
8" 45.00-57.00

T. B. Clark & Co.
MAGNOLIA
8" 210.00-240.00
9" 240.00-270.00
10" 300.00-350.00

Higgins & Seiter
WEBSTER
Fruit, Salad or Berry
8" 111.00-129.00
9" 129.00-147.00
10" 147.00-177.00

BOWLS

Pitkins & Brooks
CORSAIR SALAD
BOWL
Standard Grade
8'' 44.00-60.00
9'' 77.00-88.00

Averbeck
MARIETTA BOWL
7'' 55.50-66.50
8'' 71.50-82.50
9'' 82.50-99.50
10'' 104.50-137.50

Pitkins & Brooks
WINONA SALAD
BOWL
P & B Grade
8'' 90.00-101.00
9'' 101.00-112.00

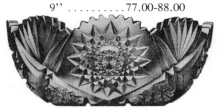

Averbeck
LIBERTY BOWL
7'' 71.50-88.50
8'' 93.50-110.50
9'' 121.50-148.50
10'' 148.50-165.50

Averbeck
GEORGIA BOWL
8'' 49.50-71.50
9'' 77.50-93.50
10'' 115.50-137.50

Averbeck
AMERICAN BEAUTY
BOWL
7'' 96.00-107.00
8'' 107.00-137.00
9'' 137.00-143.00
10'' 154.00-181.00

Pitkins & Brooks
CLARION SALAD
BOWL
P & B Grade
7'' 77.50-104.50

Averbeck
HUDSON BOWL
7'' 47.00-58.00
8'' 58.00-69.00
9'' 74.00-85.00
10'' 91.00-113.00

Pitkins & Brooks
RAJAH SALAD BOWL
P & B Grade
8'' 96.00-107.00
9'' 118.00-156.00
10'' 167.00-195.00

Pitkins & Brooks
ELSIE SALAD BOWL
P & B Grade
8'' 104.50-115.50

Averbeck
RUBY BOWL
7'' 41.00-46.00
8'' 46.00-63.00
9'' 68.00-85.00
10'' 96.00-125.00

Averbeck
CAIRO BOWL
9'' 165.00-198.00

Averbeck
LONDON
Oval Bowl or Dish
10'' 99.00-110.00

Averbeck
SPRUCE BOWL
7'' 38.50-49.50
8'' 49.50-66.50
9'' 60.50-77.50
10'' 82.50-110.50

Pitkins & Brooks
MARS SALAD BOWL
P & B Grade
8'' 55.00-77.00
9'' 88.00-110.00

BOWLS

J. D. Bergen
KENWOOD
7" 99.00-110.00
8" 110.00-126.50
9" 143.00-154.50
10" 171.00-209.00

J. D. Bergen
ELSA
7" 44.00-55.00
8" 55.00-66.00
9" 77.00-93.00
10" 121.00-154.00

J. D. Bergen
FLORENCE
5" 91.00-126.00
6" 126.00-162.00

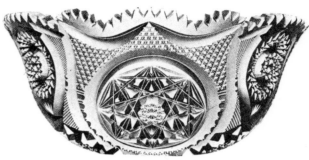

J. D. Bergen
CHESTER
7" 150.00-185.00
8" 185.00-205.00
9" 230.00-255.00
10" 325.00-425.00

Averbeck
ROOSEVELT
Oval Bowl
11½" 165.00-192.00

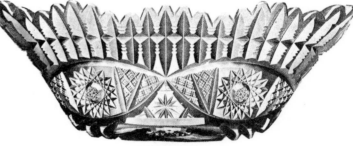

J. D. Bergen
KENWOOD
Oblong Bowl
10½" 159.00-187.00

J. D. Bergen
IVANHOE
8" 96.00-104.00
9" 110.00-129.00

J. D. Bergen
HILDA
8" 126.50-159.50

BOWLS

J. D. Bergen
AMBROSE
7" 82.50-99.50
8" 104.50-126.50
9" 132.50-159.50
10" 176.50-198.50

J. D. Bergen
GOLF
7" 44.50-49.50
8" 49.50-60.50
9" 77.50-88.50
10" 104.50-126.50

J. D. Bergen
RENWICK
7" 90.00-95.00
8" 105.00-125.00
9" 150.00-170.00
10" 180.00-200.00

J. D. Bergen
HAMPTON
7" 125.00-145.00
8" 155.00-180.00
9" 190.00-220.00
10" 220.00-245.00

J. D. Bergen
BERMUDA
7" 49.50-60.50
8" 82.50-88.50
9" 110.50-137.50
10" 148.50-181.50

J. D. Bergen
GOLDENROD
7" 55.50-66.50
8" 71.50-82.50
9" 93.50-115.50
10" 126.50-143.50

BOWLS

J. D. Bergen
MARLOW
7'' 49.50-60.50
8'' 77.50-88.50
9'' 93.50-115.50
10'' 126.50-159.50

J. D. Bergen
ST. LOUIS
7'' 77.50-82.50
8'' 99.50-104.50
9'' 126.50-137.50
10'' 148.50-170.50

J. D. Bergen
CORSAIR
7'' 66.00-77.00
8'' 82.00-93.00
9'' 104.00-121.00
10'' 143.00-170.00

J. D. Bergen
WEBSTER
7'' 82.50-92.50
8'' 97.50-107.50
9'' 117.50-137.50
10'' 142.50-177.50

J. D. Bergen
KEYSTONE
7'' 47.00-58.00
8'' 63.00-82.00
9'' 88.00-102.00
10'' 115.00-140.00

J. D. Bergen
BEDFORD
7'' 38.00-55.00
8'' 49.00-66.00
9'' 77.00-108.00
10'' 110.00-143.00

BOWLS

Averbeck
CANTON BOWL
7" 36.00-47.00
8" 52.00-69.00
9" 74.00-91.00
10" 118.00-135.00

J. D. Bergen
MAGNET
7" 38.50-49.50
8" 71.50-82.50

Averbeck
NICE BOWL
7" 100.00-120.00
8" 120.00-140.00
9" 135.00-160.00
10" 175.00-190.00

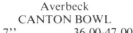

Averbeck
DAISY BOWL
7" 97.50-112.50
8" 107.50-122.50
9" 132.50-152.50
10" 152.50-182.50

Pitkins & Brooks
CLEO SALAD BOWL
P & B Grade
8" 99.00-121.00

Averbeck
FRISCO BOWL
8" 47.00-58.00
9" 69.00-80.00
10" 97.00-113.00

Averbeck
GENOA
Oval Bowl or Dish
10" 115.50-137.50

MONARCH
8" 85.00-91.00
9" 96.00-113.00
10" 124.00-135.00

Pitkins & Brooks
PINTO DISH
P & B Grade
10" 154.00-181.00

Averbeck
PUCK BOWL
8" 55.50-66.50
9" 66.50-82.50
10" 104.50-115.50

Averbeck
DIAMOND BOWL
7" 110.00-120.00
8" 120.00-135.00
9" 140.00-165.00
10" 170.00-205.00

Pitkins & Brooks
FLEUR DE LIS
SALAD BOWL
P & B Grade
8" 88.00-104.00

Pitkins & Brooks
SUNBURST FANCY
BOWL
P & B Grade
8" 124.00-135.00

Pitkins & Brooks
EMPRESS SALAD
BOWL
P & B Grade
8" 143.00-165.00
9" 165.00-187.00

Pitkins & Brooks
ORIOLE SALAD BOWL
P & B Grade
8" 55.00-82.00

BUTTER TUBS - TRAYS - BUTTERETTES

Averbeck
RUBY
Butter tub and plate
Two pieces 180.00-198.00

T. B. Clark & Co.
MANHATTAN
Butter tub and plate
Two pieces 180.00-216.00

Averbeck
NAPOLEON
Butter tub and plate
Two pieces 162.00-222.00

Averbeck
BOSTON
Butter tub and plate
Two pieces 120.00-144.00

J. D. Bergen
SEASIDE
Butter tub and plate
Two pieces 186.00-216.00

J. D. Bergen
ELECTRIC
Covered butter and plate
Two pieces 245.00-255.00

J. D. Bergen
ORLAND
Covered butter and plate
Two pieces 245.00-255.00

Higgins & Seiter
ELITE
Glass Dish
Each 51.50-63.50

J. D. Bergen
PRISM
5" 93.00-105.00
6" 117.00-129.00

J. D. Bergen
RUBY
Handled Butter Plate
5" 90.00-108.00

Averbeck
SARATOGA
Butterette
Each 22.00-24.00

Averbeck
ASHLAND
Butter Plate
Each 30.00-33.00

Averbeck
PRISCILLA
Butterette
3½" 22.00-24.00

Averbeck
LADY CURZON
Butterette
3½" 22.00-24.00

Averbeck
CANTON
Butterette
3½" 22.00-24.00

Averbeck
SPRUCE
Butterette
3½" 22.00-24.0

CANDLESTICKS

J. D. Bergen
3 LIGHT
CANDELABRA
Each 204.00-252.00

J. D. Bergen
ALBERT
10'' Candlestick
Each 174.00-192.00

J. D. Bergen
VICTORIA
Candlestick
7'' 102.00-138.00
10'' 156.00-174.00

CANDLESTICKS

Pitkins & Brooks
IMPORTED
CANDLESTICK
7½'' 36.00
9¼'' 54.00

J. D. Bergen
5 LIGHT
CANDELABRA
Each 234.00-276.00

Pitkins & Brooks
IMPORTED
CANDLESTICK
7½'' 42.00
9¼'' 54.00
10½'' 66.00

Pitkins & Brooks
ORO CANDLESTICK
P & B Grade
8'' 96.00-132.00

Pitkins & Brooks
HALLE VASE
P & B Grade
12'' 84.00
14'' 98.00
16'' 126.00
18'' 173.00

CARAFES

J. D. Bergen
GOLDENROD
Quart Carafe
Each 180.00-210.00

J. D. Bergen
ARLINGTON
Quart Carafe
Each 90.00-108.00

J. D. Bergen
PROGRESS
Quart Carafe
Each 138.00-168.00

Averbeck
NAPOLEON
Quart 60.00-72.00

Higgins & Seiter
TORNADO
Each 96.00-108.00

Higgins & Seiter
WEBSTER
Quart 72.00-90.00

Higgins & Seiter
MONARCH
Quart 138.00-180.00

J. D. Bergen
NEWPORT
Quart 99.00-114.00

J. D. Bergen
GILMORE
Quart 114.00-117.00

J. D. Bergen
METEOR
Quart 72.00-90.00

CARAFES

J. D. Bergen
GOLF
Quart 96.00-108.00

Pitkins & Brooks
WINFIELD CARAFE
Standard Grade
Globe 72.00-90.00

J. D. Bergen
WAVERLY
Quart 96.00-126.00

Averbeck
ACME
Quart 150.00-180.00

J. D. Bergen
U.S.
Quart 72.00-90.00

Averbeck
PRISM
Quart 96.00-138.00

J. D. Bergen
ANSONIA
Quart 96.00-120.00

Pitkins & Brooks
MYRTLE CARAFE
Standard Grade
Globe 96.00-114.00

J. D. Bergen
GOLDENROD
Quart 125.00-150.00

CARAFES

J. D. Bergen
COLONY
Quart 130.00-165.00

J. D. Bergen
MARIE
Quart 140.00-160.00

J. D. Bergen
NEWPORT
Quart 99.00-126.00

T. B. Clark & Co.
MANHATTAN
Quart 85.00-96.00

T. B. Clark & Co.
MANHATTAN
Priscilla Carafe
Each 185.00-210.00

T. B. Clark & Co.
WINOLA
Quart 71.00-88.00

T. B. Clark & Co.
JEWEL
Quart 77.00-88.00

J. D. Bergen
ROLAND
Quart 99.00-110.00

J. D. Bergen
BEDFORD
Quart 77.00-82.00

J. D. Bergen
BALTIMORE
Quart 88.00-93.00

CARAFES

J. D. Bergen
ANSONIA
Quart 69.00-85.00

J. D. Bergen
BEDFORD
Quart 71.00-88.00

J. D. Bergen
WAVERLY
Quart 82.50-137.50

Higgins & Seiter
DIAMOND FAN
Quart 44.00-66.00

T. B. Clark & Co.
WINOLA
Quart 77.00-88.00

Higgins & Seiter
KENMORE
Quart 47.00-71.00

T. B. Clark & Co.
HENRY VIII
Quart 91.00-107.00

J. D. Bergen
ATLAS
Quart 77.00-99.00

J. D. Bergen
U.S.
Quart 66.00-85.00

J. D. Bergen
ORIENT
Quart 77.00-104.00

CARAFES

Pitkins & Brooks
RAJAH GLOBE
P & B Grade
Each 125.00-150.00

Pitkins & Brooks
VENICE CARAFE
Standard Grade
Each 77.00-99.00

Pitkins & Brooks
MARS CARAFE
P & B Grade
Quart 132.00-159.00

Pitkins & Brooks
HEART GLOBE
P & B Grade
Each 140.00-160.00

Averbeck
LIBERTY
Quart 132.00-159.00

Pitkins & Brooks
MEADVILLE CARAFE
Standard Grade
Each 88.00-110.00

T. B. Clark & Co.
MANHATTAN
Quart 88.00-99.00

Averbeck
DAISY
Quart 126.50-148.50

Pitkins & Brooks
SUNBURST
P & B Grade
Each 121.00-148.00

Pitkins & Brooks
CAROLYN GLOBE
P & B Grade
Each 110.00-137.00

Pitkins & Brooks
BELMONT GLOBE
P & B Grade
Each 121.00-148.00

Pitkins & Brooks
CRETE
P & B Grade
Each 99.00-115.00

CARAFES

Pitkins & Brooks
MEADVILLE
Standard Grade
Each 71.50-82.50

Averbeck
GEORGIA
Quart 77.00-88.00

Averbeck
BOSTON
Quart 99.00-137.00

Averbeck
FLORIDA
Quart 99.00-137.00

Averbeck
LADY CURZON
Quart 71.00-99.00

Pitkins & Brooks
IMPORTED
Each 60.00-88.00

Averbeck
RADIUM
Quart 79.00-96.00

Averbeck
VIENNA
Quart 82.00-99.00

Averbeck
TRIXY
Quart 82.00-99.00

Averbeck
MAUD ADAMS
Quart 125.00-150.00

Averbeck
MELBA
Quart 88.00-110.00

CELERY DIPS, SALT DIPS, KNIFE RESTS

Pitkins & Brooks
CELERY DIPS
2" 24.00

Pitkins & Brooks
CELERY DIPS
1½" 18.00

Pitkins & Brooks
CELERY DIPS
1-5/8" 16.50

Pitkins & Brooks
CELERY DIPS
2" 11.00

Pitkins & Brooks
CELERY DIPS
1¾" 20.00

Pitkins & Brooks
CELERY DIPS
1-7/8" 14.00

Pitkins & Brooks
CELERY DIPS
1½" 15.50

Pitkins & Brooks
CELERY DIPS, OVAL
1-7/8" 12.00

Pitkins & Brooks
TABLE SALT
2½" 15.50

Pitkins & Brooks
TABLE SALT
AMELIA
3-1/8" 15.50

T. B. Clark & Co.
VENUS
Nest Table Salt
Each 15.50

J. D. Bergen
DeSOTO
Pair 36.00

J. D. Bergen
SUPERIOR
Each 16.00

J. D. Bergen
Round Salt
2" 14.00
2¼" 15.00
2½" 18.00
2¾" 22.00

Pitkins & Brooks
KNIFE RESTS
3½" 31.00
4½" 33.00
6" 49.50

Pitkins & Brooks
KNIFE RESTS
3½" 38.50
4½" 55.00
5½" 71.50

Pitkins & Brooks
KNIFE RESTS
3¼" 33.00
4¼" 38.50
5" 60.50

J. D. Bergen
KNIFE RESTS
Ind., Pair 34.00
Med., pair 38.50
Lg., pair 51.75

Pitkins & Brooks
HEXAGON KNIFE
RESTS
Standard Grade
4" 24.00

J. D. Bergen
KNIFE RESTS
2½", pair 24.00
3¼", pair 32.00
5", pair 38.50

CELERY TRAYS

T. B. Clark & Co.
DORRANCE
Each 60.00-72.00

Higgins & Seiter
WEBSTER
11½'' 72.00-96.00

T. B. Clark & Co.
WINOLA
Each 78.00-108.00

Higgins & Seiter
AETNA
4½''x12'' 54.00-66.00

Higgins & Seiter
DELHI
4½''x11¾'' . . . 48.00-60.00

T. B. Clark & Co.
NORDICA
Each 48.00-60.00

J. D. Bergen
STANLEY
6''x12'' 144.00-180.00

J. D. Bergen
MADISON
4½''x11¾'' 66.00-90.00

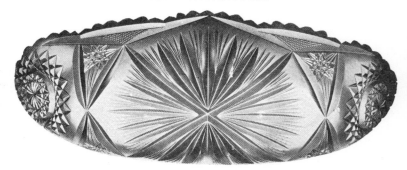

J. D. Bergen
DIADEM
5''x11'' . . . 90.00-120.00

J. D. Bergen
GOLDENROD
5''x11'' 90.00-120.00

CELERY TRAYS

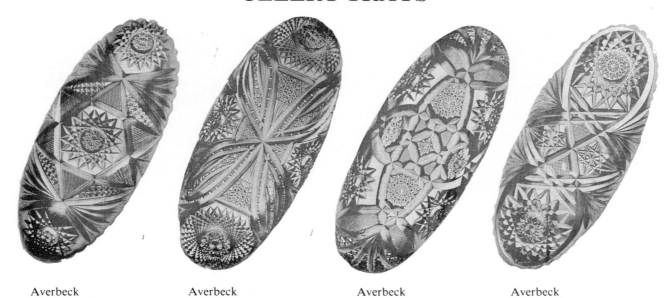

Averbeck
FLEUR DE LIS
11¼" 66.00-88.00

Averbeck
DIAMOND
12" 99.00-143.00

Averbeck
LIBERTY
11¼" 77.00-99.00

Averbeck
RUBY
11¼" 77.00-99.00

Averbeck
LIBERTY
12" 96.00-126.00

Averbeck
FRISCO
12" 96.00-126.00

Averbeck
DIAMOND
11¾" 115.00-143.00

Higgins & Seiter
ST. CLOUD
4"x11½" 55.00-85.00

T. B. Clark & Co.
MANHATTAN
Each 104.50-137.50

CELERY TRAYS

Pitkins & Brooks
HALLE
P & B Grade
11½" 77.00-99.00

Pitkins & Brooks
BOWA
P & B Grade
12" 88.00-110.00

Averbeck
LADY CURZON
11¼" 66.00-77.00

Averbeck
FRISCO
11¼" 66.00-82.00

Averbeck
AMERICAN BEAUTY
11¼" 74.00-96.00

Averbeck
EMPRESS
11¼" 91.00-113.00

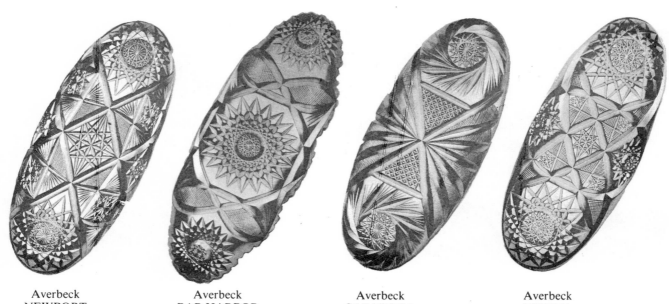

Averbeck
NEWPORT
11¼" 66.00-82.00

Averbeck
BAR HARBOR
11¼" 71.00-88.00

Averbeck
SARATOGA
11¼" 66.00-93.00

Averbeck
VIENNA
11¼" 88.00-93.00

CELERY TRAYS

Pitkins & Brooks
RAJAH
P & B Grade
11¾" 93.50-137.50

Pitkins & Brooks
VENICE
P & B Grade
Each 88.00-110.00

Pitkins & Brooks
MARS
P & B Grade
10¾" 93.00-121.00

Pitkins & Brooks
RAJAH FANCY
P & B Grade
11½" 145.00-180.00

Pitkins & Brooks
MEADVILLE
Standard Grade
11" 93.50-126.50

Pitkins & Brooks
ORIOLE
P & B Grade
Each 88.00-121.00

Pitkins & Brooks
ATHOLE
P & B Grade
12" 93.00-121.00

Pitkins & Brooks
EMPRESS
P & B Grade
Each 104.00-132.00

Pitkins & Brooks
PLYMOUTH
P & B Grade
12" 225.00-240.00

Pitkins & Brooks
CORTEZ
P & B Grade
11" 121.00-143.00

CELERY TRAYS

J. D. Bergen
EMBLEM
4½''x11½'' 66.00-75.00

J. D. Bergen
PREMIER
5''x11'' 71.50-82.50

J. D. Bergen
OTHELLO
4½''x11¾'' 63.00-80.00

J. D. Bergen
ADELPHI
6''x13'' 125.00-175.00

T. B. Clark & Co.
DESDEMONA
Each 49.50-59.50

J. D. Bergen
GROVE
6''x13'' 110.00-126.00

Higgins & Seiter
ARLINGTON
11½''x4¼'' 44.00-60.00

T. B. Clark & Co.
ADONIS
Each 55.00-65.00

Higgins & Seiter
5½''x12'' 65.00-80.00

CELERY TRAYS

J. D. Bergen
BELVIDERE
5''x11'' 121.00-137.00

Pitkins & Brooks
MYRTLE
11'' 77.00-93.00

J. D. Bergen
SHARON
4¾''x12½'' . . . 88.00-132.00

J. D. Bergen
CAPRICE
5½''x12'' 132.00-148.00

J. D. Bergen
HAVEN
5''x12'' 95.00-100.00

J. D. Bergen
DOMINO
4½''x11'' . . . 95.00-100.00

Pitkins & Brooks
NELLORE
P & B Grade
Each 121.00-165.00

J. D. Bergen
EMERSON
6''x12'' 210.00-250.00

CHEESE PLATES and MAYONNAISE SETS

Higgins & Seiter
WEBSTER
Complete . . 265.00-280.00

T. B. Clark & Co.
MANHATTAN
Cheese Cover and Plate
Complete . . 255.00-305.00

Higgins & Seiter
NEW YORK
9" 215.00-255.00
10" 235.00-280.00

J. D. Bergen
GLENWOOD
5" 275.00-295.00
6" 290.00-315.00

J. D. Bergen
IRENE
Whipped Cream Bowl
3 Handled
6" 115.00-130.00

Averbeck
GEORGIA
Mayonnaise Set
Bowl and Plate
Set 75.00-90.00

Higgins & Seiter
NAPOLEON
Bowl and Plate
Set 90.00-100.00

J. D. Bergen
BURLINGTON
Whipped Cream Bowl
6" 95.00-105.00

Averbeck
RADIUM
Mayonnaise Set
Bowl and Plate
5" 85.00-105.00

Averbeck
LIBERTY
Mayonnaise Bowl
Each 75.00-90.00

Higgins & Seiter
FLORENTINE
Mayonnaise Set
Bowl and Plate
6" 85.00-105.00

Higgins & Seiter
IMPERIAL
Mayonnaise Set
Bowl and Tray
Set 75.00-90.00

CIGAR JARS

Pitkins & Brooks
ZESTA CIGAR JAR
P & B Grade
8½'' 230.00-255.00

Higgins & Seiter
CIGAR JAR
Top made hollow for
holding sponge.
50 white . . .140.00-165.00
25 white . . .125.00-135.00
50 green . . .165.00-190.00
25 green . . .140.00-160.00

Higgins & Seiter
CIGAR JAR
With frame in either
mahogany or antique oak
50 Cigars 330.00-355.00

Higgins & Seiter
MAJESTIC
6½'' 170.00-200.00

Higgins & Seiter
RENAISSANCE
Top made hollow for
holding sponge.
50 white . . .155.00-180.00
25 white . . .125.00-150.00
50 green . . .180.00-205.00
25 green . . .150.00-175.00

J. D. Bergen
GLENWOOD
50 Cigars . .275.00-305.00
Cigarette . . .230.00-275.00

Higgins & Seiter
Top made hollow for
inserting sponge.
50 white . . .155.00-180.00
25 white . . .140.00-150.00
50 green . . .180.00-205.00
25 green . . .155.00-175.00

J. D. Bergen
SEASIDE
25 Cigars . .165.00-190.00

TOBACCO JARS and COLOGNE BOTTLES

J. D. Bergen
WAGNER
Cologne

7" 55.00
7½" 63.00
8½" 70.00

J. D. Bergen
PREMIER
Tobacco Jar
7½" 230.00-280.00

J. D. Bergen
MEDORA
Cologne

7" 45.00
7½" 55.00
8½" 70.00

Pitkins & Brooks
IMPORTED COLOGNE
3 oz. 35.00
7 oz. 45.00
9 oz. 51.00

Pitkins & Brooks
ENO COLOGNE
P & B Grade
4 oz. 46.00
6 oz. 56.00
8 oz. 68.00

J. D. Bergen
PREMIER
Cologne

5" 35.00
6" 42.00
7" 54.00
8" 65.00

J. D. Bergen
PRISM
Cologne

7" 41.00
8" 47.00
9" 55.00

Averbeck
RADIUM
Cologne

3½" 27.00
4½" 31.00
5½" 34.00

Pitkins & Brooks
SUNBURST COLOGNE
P & B Grade
6 oz. 28.00
8 oz. 31.00

Pitkins & Brooks
CAROLYN COLOGNE
P & B Grade
6 oz. 28.00

Pitkins & Brooks
IMPORTED
COLOGNE
3 oz. 25.00
5 oz. 27.00

Pitkins & Brooks
IMPORTED
COLOGNE
3 oz. 25.00
5 oz. 27.00
8 oz. 34.00

COLOGNE BOTTLES

Pitkins & Brooks
BERRIE COLOGNE
P & B Grade
oz. 32.00
oz. 37.00

Pitkins & Brooks
BERRIE COLOGNE
P & B Grade
5 oz. 37.00

Pitkins & Brooks
AURORA BOREALIS
COLOGNE
P & B Grade
6 oz. 44.00

Pitkins & Brooks
ELECTRA TOILET
WATER BOTTLE
P & B Grade
8 oz. 42.00

Pitkins & Brooks
KING GEORGE
COLOGNE
P & B Grade
8 oz. 41.00

Pitkins & Brooks
BERMUDA COLOGNE
P & B Grade
6 oz. 40.00

Pitkins & Brooks
PRISM RUM BOTTLE
P & B Grade
9½'' 47.00-54.00

Pitkins & Brooks
MARS COLOGNE
P & B Grade
6 oz. 37.00
8 oz. 48.00

Pitkins & Brooks
HALLE COLOGNE
P & B Grade
6 oz. 34.00
10 oz. 47.00

Pitkins & Brooks
BELMONT COLOGNE
P & B Grade
6 oz. 35.00
10 oz. 43.00

T. B. Clark & Co.
SQUARE COLOGNE
ST. GEORGE
8 oz. 45.00-49.00
12 oz. 53.00-57.00

T. B. Clark & Co.
ROUND COLOGNE
JEWEL
6 oz. 29.00
8 oz. 33.00
12 oz. 41.00

T. B. Clark & Co.
GLOBE COLOGNE,
JEWEL
6 oz. 28.00
9 oz. 33.00
18 oz. 54.00
24 oz. 74.00

Higgins & Seiter
ST. JULIEN
4 oz. 25.00
6 oz. 28.00
8 oz. 31.00
12 oz. 36.00

COMB and BRUSH TRAYS,
PIN HOLDERS, POMADE JARS

Pitkins & Brooks
ELECTRA COMB &
BRUSH TRAY
P & B Grade
11" 189.00-289.00

Pitkins & Brooks
ALADDIN COMB &
BRUSH TRAY
P & B Grade
12" 210.00-247.00

Pitkins & Brooks
DELMAR COMB &
BRUSH TRAY
P & B Grade
11" 178.00-247.00

Pitkins & Brooks
ELECTRA POMADE
BOX
P & B Grade
2¾" 42.00-52.00

J. D. Bergen
PRISM
Pomade Jar
Each 42.00-52.00

Averbeck
RUBY
Pin or Olive Tray
Each 52.50-82.50

Pitkins & Brooks
ELECTRA HAT PIN
HOLDER
P & B Grade
7" 47.50

J. D. Bergen
SPLIT & HOLLOW
Pin Tray
Each 62.50-72.50

COMPOTES

J. D. Bergen
BERMUDA
High footed Comport
8'' 205.00-230.00

Pitkins & Brooks
EMPIRE FOOTED
BOWL
P & B Grade
(2 pieces)
Set 255.00-280.00

Averbeck
VIENNA
Each 205.00-215.00

Pitkins & Brooks
MEMPHIS
5'' (across top) . . .155.00-165.00
6''   ''   '' . . .180.00-190.00
7''   ''   '' . . .195.00-210.00

Pitkins & Brooks
HEART
P & B Grade
9''x5'' 175.00-185.00

Pitkins & Brooks
CRETE
P & B Grade
5'' 110.00-140.00

Averbeck
RADIUM
Bon Bon with Foot
6'' 150.00-155.00

Pitkins & Brooks
MARS FOOTED
FRUIT BOWL
P & B Grade
8'' 180.00-190.00

Averbeck
LONDON
Spoon dish with foot
7½'' 155.00-170.00

COMPOTES

Pitkins & Brooks
HURON
P & B Grade
Each 95.00-105.00

Pitkins & Brooks
HEART
P & B Grade
7½'' 110.00-115.00

Pitkins & Brooks
SAVANNAH COMPORT
ENGRAVED
P & B Grade
7'' 110.00-140.00

Pitkins & Brooks
AUTO COMPORT
P & B Grade
Each 150.00-185.00

Pitkins & Brooks
HALLE COMPORT
P & B Grade
5'' 80.00-95.00

Pitkins & Brooks
MYRTLE COMPORT
Standard Grade
5'' 80.00-90.00
7'' 115.00-130.00

Pitkins & Brooks
McKINLEY COMPORT
P & B Grade
7'' 150.00-185.00

Pitkins & Brooks
TOPAZ COMPORT
P & B Grade
9''x6'' 150.00-185.00

Pitkins & Brooks
GLEE COMPORT
P & B Grade
8''x7½'' . . .195.00-215.00

46

COMPOTES

Averbeck
NAPLES
9½" 150.00-170.00

Averbeck
GEORGIA
Each 182.50-237.50

Averbeck
DIAMOND
Each 200.50-220.50

Averbeck
NICE
10¼" 147.00-185.00

Pitkins & Brooks
ATLAS
12"x6" 192.50-220.50

Pitkins & Brooks
HALLE COMPORT
P & B Grade
Each 137.50-152.50

Pitkins & Brooks
RAJAH
P & B Grade
8" 150.00-155.00
10" 165.00-180.00
12" 195.00-215.00
14" 230.00-255.00

Pitkins & Brooks
ALEXIS
P & B Grade
Each 85.00-105.00

Averbeck
MAUD ADAMS
Each 85.00-105.00

Pitkins & Brooks
VILLA
P & B Grade
5" 55.00-80.00

COMPOTES

Pitkins & Brooks
ZELLER
P & B Grade
7''x5'' 45.00-55.00

J. D. Bergen
MAGNET
5'' 45.00-55.00
6'' 55.00-65.00

Pitkins & Brooks
ATLAS
P & B Grade
9''x6'' 155.00-180.00

J. D. Bergen
BEACON
6'' 95.00-110.00

J. D. Bergen
ENTERPRISE
6'' 100.00-110.00
7'' 110.00-120.00
8'' 120.00-130.00
9'' 140.00-155.00
10'' 165.00-195.00

Averbeck
LIBERTY
Each 135.00-145.00

J. D. Bergen
WALTHAM
6'' 95.00-110.00

Pitkins & Brooks
BORDER
(2 handled)
P & B Grade
10'' 205.00-230.00

Averbeck
LONDON
Each 180.00-205.00

Pitkins & Brooks
CRESS
P & B Grade
5'' 95.00-100.00
6'' 100.00-125.00

Pitkins & Brooks
SEPIA
P & B Grade
Each 95.00-105.00

Averbeck
TRIXY
Each 87.00-92.00

Pitkins & Brooks
IMPORTED COMPORT
5'' 35.00-40.00
6'' 40.00-50.00
7'' 50.00-60.00
8'' 80.00-90.00

COMPOTES

J. D. Bergen
MARCUS
7" 155.00-165.00
8" 165.00-190.00
9" 210.00-240.00

J. D. Bergen
CARMEN
High Foot Comport
Each 165.00-175.00
Each 190.00-215.00
Each 240.00-305.00
(Original catalaog did not
have sizes listed)

T. B. Clark & Co.
MANHATTAN
6" 82.00-90.00

J. D. Bergen
WATSON
6" 140.00-150.00
7" 155.00-165.00
8" 175.00-190.00
9" 190.00-240.00

J. D. Bergen
ARCADIA
Each 215.00-265.00

CORDIAL SETS and WHISKEY SETS

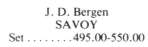

J. D. Bergen
SAVOY
Set 495.00-550.00

J. D. Bergen
GLENWOOD
Set 330.00-355.00

J. D. Bergen
PREMIER
Set 300.00-350.00

CORDIAL SETS and WHISKEY SETS

J. D. Bergen
GLENWOOD
Set 285.00-355.00

J. D. Bergen
GLENWOOD
Set 295.00-355.00

J. D. Bergen
ELECTRIC
Set 225.00-275.00

J. D. Bergen
ELECTRIC
Set 125.00-275.00

CORDIAL SETS and WHISKEY SETS

Higgins & Seiter
WEBSTER
Set 187.00-225.00

Higgins & Seiter
SYROTT
Set 187.50-237.50

Higgins & Seiter
CONCORD
Set 225.00-250.00

Higgins & Seiter
MANILLA
Set 150.00-195.00

Higgins & Seiter
COLONIAL
Set 125.50-150.50

Higgins & Seiter
HENRIETTA
Set 125.00-160.00

CORDIAL SETS and WHISKEY SETS

Higgins & Seiter
GEORGIA
2 bottles 325.00-375.00
3 bottles 425.00-525.00

Higgins & Seiter
DEWEY
2 bottles 330.00-355.00

CREAM and SUGAR

J. D. Bergen
GLENWOOD
Cream 66.00-82.00

J. D. Bergen
GLENWOOD
Sugar 77.00-88.00

J. D. Bergen
DETROIT
Half Pint Footed
Cream 44.00-75.00

J. D. Bergen
OREGON
Half Pint
Cream 49.50-59.50

J. D. Bergen
DETROIT
Footed
Sugar 60.00-80.00

J. D. Bergen
GOLF
Sugar 45.00-55.00

J. D. Bergen
GILBERT
Sugar 55.00-65.00

J. D. Bergen
SUPERIOR
Half Pint
Cream 55.00-70.00

J. D. Bergen
MAGNET
Sugar 40.00-55.00

Higgins & Seiter
ARLINGTON
Sugar and Creamer
Set 55.00-65.00

Higgins & Seiter
WASHINGTON
Sugar and Creamer
Set 35.00-50.00

Higgins & Seiter
WEBSTER
Sugar and Creamer
Set 50.00-60.00

Higgins & Seiter
BELVEDERE
Sugar and Creamer
Set 50.00-60.00

CREAM and SUGAR

J. D. Bergen
GOLF
Half Pint Cream
Each 37.50-47.50

J. D. Bergen
AVON
Sugar 45.00-60.00

J. D. Bergen
EMBLEM
Sugar 35.00-50.00

J. D. Bergen
AVON
Cream 47.50-57.50

J. D. Bergen
GILBERT
Half Pint Cream
Each 55.00-70.00

J. D. Bergen
GOLF
Half Pint Cream
Each 55.00-70.00

J. D. Bergen
EMBLEM
Half Pint Cream
Each 42.50-52.50

J. D. Bergen
MAGNET
Half Pint Cream
Each 45.00-55.00

J. D. Bergen
GRACE
Half Pint Cream
Each 40.00-55.00

J. D. Bergen
GRACE
Sugar 45.00-52.00

J. D. Bergen
GOLF
Sugar 50.00-65.00

J. D. Bergen
SUPERIOR
Sugar 50.00-70.00

J. D. Bergen
OREGON
Sugar 37.00-50.00

J. D. Bergen
BEDFORD
Half Pint Cream
Each 40.00-55.00

J. D. Bergen
BEDFORD
Sugar 50.00-75.00

CREAM and SUGAR

Averbeck
MELBA
Cream and Sugar
Set 82.00-110.00

Averbeck
GEORGIA
Cream and Sugar
Set 82.00-95.00

Averbeck
SARATOGA
Cream and Sugar
Set 110.00-120.00

Averbeck
LIBERTY
Cream and Sugar
Set 88.00-125.00

Averbeck
VIENNA
Cream and Sugar
Set 110.00-120.00

Averbeck
FLORIDA
Cream and Sugar
Set 77.00-95.00

Averbeck
LADY CURZON
Cream and Sugar
Set 82.00-110.00

Averbeck
RUBY
Cream and Sugar
Set 77.00-90.00

Averbeck
LIBERTY
Cream and Sugar
Set 132.00-195.00

Averbeck
AMERICAN BEAUTY
Cream and Sugar
Set 165.00-205.00

Averbeck
PRISCILLA
Cream and Sugar
Set 82.00-99.00

Averbeck
RUBY
Half Pint Cream
Each 55.00-66.00

Averbeck
FLORIDA
Cream and Sugar
Set 66.00-92.00

CREAM and SUGAR

Pitkins & Brooks
BORDER
SUGAR & CREAM
P & B Grade
Set 132.50-157.50

Pitkins & Brooks
SUNBURST
SUGAR & CREAM
P & B Grade
Set 145.00-172.00

Pitkins & Brooks
CAROLYN
P & B Grade
Set 130.00-140.00

Pitkins & Brooks
RAJAH
P & B Grade
Set 137.50-147.50

Pitkins & Brooks
TRIUMPH
P & B Grade
Set 82.50-87.50

Pitkins & Brooks
MEADVILLE
Standard Grade
Set 55.00-80.00

Pitkins & Brooks
PLYMOUTH
P & B Grade
Set 185.00-195.00

Pitkins & Brooks
DUCHESS
P & B Grade
Set 185.00-210.00

Pitkins & Brooks
GARLAND
P & B Grade
Set 120.00-142.00

Pitkins & Brooks
PRISM
P & B Grade
Set 99.00-132.00

CREAM and SUGAR

Pitkins & Brooks ORIOLE P & B Grade Set 68.00-89.00	Pitkins & Brooks MYRTLE Standard Grade Set 58.00-80.00

Pitkins & Brooks BYRNS P & B Grade Set 96.00-107.00	Pitkins & Brooks MARS P & B Grade Set 76.00-92.00

Pitkins & Brooks HALLE P & B Grade Set 92.00-103.00	Pitkins & Brooks VENICE P & B Grade Set 59.50-70.50

Pitkins & Brooks BELMONT P & B Grade Set 104.00-126.00	Pitkins & Brooks NORTHERN STAR P & B Grade Set 85.00-102.00

Pitkins & Brooks ORIOLE P & B Grade Set 52.00-58.00	Pitkins & Brooks HEART P & B Grade Set 126.00-154.00

CREAM and SUGAR

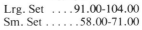
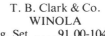

T. B. Clark & Co.
VENUS
Set 154.00-181.00

T. B. Clark & Co.
WINOLA
Lrg. Set 91.00-104.00
Sm. Set 58.00-71.00

Higgins & Seiter
ARLINGTON
Set 47.00-60.00

T. B. Clark & Co.
ARBUTUS
Set 52.00-63.00

CUPS

Averbeck
VIENNA
Cup 30.00-38.00

J. D. Bergen
ELECTRIC
Cup 24.00-31.00

J. D. Bergen
GOLF
Cup 24.00-31.00

J. D. Bergen
WABASH
Cup 31.00-36.00

J. D. Bergen
KENWOOD
Cup 53.00-82.00

J. D. Bergen
PREMIER
Cup 31.00-42.00

T. B. Clark & Co.
Punch Cup & Plate
Set 49.00-69.00

T. B. Clark & Co.
WINOLA
Cup 25.00-31.00

T. B. Clark & Co.
Handled Lemonades
Cup 31.00-36.00

CRUETS and OIL BOTTLES

J. D. Bergen
OREGON
Half Pint Oil
Each 52.00-63.00

J. D. Bergen
GOLF
Half Pint Oil
Each 69.00-85.00

J. D. Bergen
WAVERLY
Half Pint Oil
Each 88.00-104.00

J. D. Bergen
WAVERLY
Half Pint Oil
Each 71.00-80.00

J. D. Bergen
GARLAND
Half Pint Cruet
Each 55.00-69.00

J. D. Bergen
WAVERLY
Third pt. 49.50-60.50
Half pt. 71.50-82.50

Pitkins & Brooks
GARLAND OIL
Each 35.00-47.00

Pitkins & Brooks
IMPORTER OIL
Each 25.00-31.00

Pitkins & Brooks
IMPORTED OIL
Each 18.00-24.00

J. D. Bergen
VIOLA
Half Pint Cruet
Each 60.00-74.00

J. D. Bergen
PRISM
Half Pint Oil
Each 31.00-35.00

J. D. Bergen
PALACE
Half Pint Oil
Each 60.00-74.00

CRUETS and OIL BOTTLES

Pitkins & Brooks
IMPORTED OIL
Each 52.00-64.00

Averbeck
FLORIDA
7½" 69.00-82.00

Pitkins & Brooks
IMPORTED OIL
6" 64.00-74.00

Pitkins & Brooks
MIKADO SQUAT OIL
P & B Grade
6" 64.00-74.00

Higgins & Seiter
PRISM
5" 36.00-47.00

Higgins & Seiter
NAPOLEON
Half pt. 52.00-64.00

Higgins & Seiter
STRAWBERRY
DIAMOND & FAN
Half pt. 52.00-64.00

Pitkins & Brooks
IMPORTED OIL
" 20.00-26.00

Higgins & Seiter
NAPOLEON
Each 47.00-58.00

Higgins & Seiter
WEBSTER
Each 30.00-41.00

T. B. Clark & Co.
MANHATTAN
Each 33.00-47.00

T. B. Clark & Co.
HURON
Each 32.00-41.00

Pitkins & Brooks
STANDARD OIL
7" 30.00-44.00

Pitkins & Brooks
IMPORTED OIL
6" 20.00-26.00

Pitkins & Brooks
IMPORTED OIL
6" 24.00-31.00

Pitkins & Brooks
BALTIC SQUAT OIL
Standard Grade
Plain handle
Each 38.00-44.00
Cut handle
Each 44.00-52.00

Pitkins & Brooks
BERMUDA OIL
P & B Grade
8½" 88.00-115.00

CRUETS and OIL BOTTLES

J. D. Bergen
GOLF
Third Pint Oil
Each 41.00-47.00

Pitkins & Brooks
KING GEORGE OIL
P & B Grade
Each 74.00-88.00

Pitkins & Brooks
RICHELIEU OIL
9¾" 31.00-41.00

Pitkins & Brooks
ALADDIN OIL
P & B Grade
Each 75.00-99.00

J. D. Bergen
ELECTRIC
Half Pint Oil
Each 52.00-66.00

Pitkins & Brooks
SUNRAY GLOBE
Standard Grade
Each 31.00-41.00

Higgins & Seiter
FLORENTINE
Each 26.00-31.00

Higgins & Seiter
CUBA
Half Pint Oil
Each 24.00-31.00

Higgins & Seiter
Each 33.00-47.00

Pitkins & Brooks
IMPORTED OIL
7½" 24.00-42.00

J. D. Bergen
PREMIER
Third pt. 49.50-60.50
Half pt. 60.50-71.50

Pitkins & Brooks
SQUAT OIL
6" 60.50-71.50

Pitkins & Brooks
IMPORTED OIL
6" 24.00-31.00

J. D. Bergen
BERKSHIRE
Third pt. 24.00-31.00
Half pt. 60.50-71.50

CUPS

Pitkins & Brooks
Standard Grade
11.00-13.00

Pitkins & Brooks
Standard Grade
46.00-51.00

Pitkins & Brooks
36.00-41.00

Pitkins & Brooks
Standard Grade
49.50-60.50

Pitkins & Brooks
P & B Grade
26.00-32.00

Pitkins & Brooks
Standard Grade
22.00-27.00

Pitkins & Brooks
SUNBURST
P & B Grade
49.50-60.50

Pitkins & Brooks
P & B Grade
49.50-60.50

Pitkins & Brooks
11.00-13.00

Pitkins & Brooks
Standard Grade
9.00-11.00

Pitkins & Brooks
GARLAND
P & B Grade
49.50-60.50

Pitkins & Brooks
9.00-11.00

Pitkins & Brooks
CAROLYN
P & B Grade
36.00-41.00

Pitkins & Brooks
MARS
P & B Grade
41.00-41.00

Pitkins & Brooks
HALLE
P & B Grade
41.00-48.00

Pitkins & Brooks
BELMONT
P & B Grade
41.00-49.00

Pitkins & Brooks
RAJAH
P & B Grade
46.00-51.00

Pitkins & Brooks
P & B Grade
41.00-48.00

Pitkins & Brooks
ORIOLE
P & B Grade
31.00-33.00

Pitkins & Brooks
HEART
P & B Grade
46.00-51.00

Pitkins & Brooks
MEADVILLE
Standard Grade
36.00-41.00

Pitkins & Brooks
RAJAH
P & B Grade
46.00-51.00

Averbeck
TRIXY
46.00-51.00

J. D. Bergen
MARLOW
33.00-38.00

J. D. Bergen
CONSAIR
33.00-38.00

J. D. Bergen
PROGRESS
36.00-41.00

J. D. Bergen
EDNA
31.00-33.00

J. D. Bergen
WABASH
33.00-44.00

Averbeck
OCCIDENT
46.00-55.00

J. D. Bergen
ELECTRIC
31.00-33.00

J. D. Bergen
MONTICELLO
36.00-41.00

J. D. Bergen
PREMIER
33.00-38.00

DECANTERS and JUGS

J. D. Bergen
GLENWOOD
1 Qt. 218.00-240.00

J. D. Bergen
ANSONIA
1 Qt. 173.00-228.00

J. D. Bergen
MARIE
1 Qt. 330.00-385.00

J. D. Bergen
ELECTRIC
1 Qt. 121.00-165.00

J. D. Bergen
GOLF
1 Pt. 107.00-143.00

Averbeck
ACME
9¼" 192.00-203.00

Averbeck
ALABAMA
1 Qt. 165.00-214.00

DECANTERS and JUGS

J. D. Bergen
GOLF
1 Pt. 143.00-192.00
1 Qt. 165.00-203.00

J. D. Bergen
ELECTRIC
1 Pt. 192.00-209.00
1 Qt. 209.00-247.00

J. D. Bergen
ELECTRIC
1 Pt. 154.00-176.00
1 Qt. 187.00-209.00

J. D. Bergen
SAVOY
1 Pt. 121.00-148.00
1 Qt. 132.00-165.00

J. D. Bergen
GOLF
1 Pt. 96.50-115.50
1 Qt. 115.50-137.50

J. D. Bergen
ANSONIA
1 Qt. 173.00-209.00

65

DECANTERS and JUGS

Pitkins & Brooks
GARLAND
1 Qt. 425.00-450.00

J. D. Bergen
SAVOY
1 Pt. 102.00-140.00
1 Qt. 162.00-192.00

J. D. Bergen
ALBERT
1 Pt. 93.50-132.50
1 Qt. 137.50-165.00

J. D. Bergen
BEAUMONT
1 Pt. 150.00-175.00

Averbeck
RADIUM
1 Pt. 99.00-132.00
1 Qt. 132.00-165.00

J. D. Bergen
CLARION
1 Qt. 150.00-200.00

Pitkins & Brooks
KING GEORGE
P & B Grade
Each 99.00-137.00

DECANTERS and JUGS

J. D. Bergen
MARIE
1 Qt. 140.00-175.00

Pitkins & Brooks
ALADDIN
P & B Grade
Each 147.00-165.00

J. D. Bergen
ASHTON
1 Qt. 147.00-180.00

J. D. Bergen
SAVOY
3 Pt. 200.00-247.00

J. D. Bergen
GLENWOOD
1 Qt. 140.00-195.00

Pitkins & Brooks
DELMAR
P & B Grade
Each 110.00-145.00

Averbeck
GENOA
Each 170.00-195.00

J. D. Bergen
GLENWOOD
1 Qt. 180.00-195.00

DECANTERS and JUGS

Higgins & Seiter
GEORGIA
13" 110.00-143.00

Higgins & Seiter
Decanter 150.00-175.00
Claret jug 160.00-195.00

Higgins & Seiter
ELECTRIC
15" 143.00-198.00

Higgins & Seiter
ELECTRIC
15" 165.00-198.00

T. B. Clark & Co.
WIDE MOUTH JUG
JEWEL
½ Pt. 49.50-60.50
Pt. 60.50-71.50
Qt. 66.50-82.50
3 Pt. 88.50-104.50
½ Gal. 104.50-137.50

Higgins & Seiter
RENAISSANCE
White 77.00-96.00
Green or Ruby 110.00-165.00

Higgins & Seiter
YACHT SHAPE
White 55.00-66.00
Green 71.00-77.00
Ruby 82.00-99.00

Pitkins & Brooks
DELMAR
P & B Grade
Each 150.00-200.00

Pitkins & Brooks
ELECTRA
P & B Grade
Qt. 150.00-195.00

J. D. Bergen
GOLF
½ Pt. 55.00-71.00

Higgins & Seiter
NAPOLEON
Pt. 44.00-55.00
Qt. 66.00-77.00
Pt. Claret 82.00-99.00
Qt. Claret . .104.00-115.00

Higgins & Seiter
FLORENTINE
Clarets 137.00-154.00
Wines 110.00-132.00
Sherries 110.00-132.00

68

DECANTERS and JUGS

Averbeck
LIBERTY
9¼" 121.00-148.00

Higgins & Seiter
FLORENTINE
Each 123.00-140.00

Higgins & Seiter
STRAWBERRY
DIAMOND FAN
½ Pt. 49.50-60.50
Pt. 60.50-71.50
Qt. 71.50-82.50
½ Pt. Claret 71.50-82.50
Pt. Claret 77.50-88.50
Qt. Claret 82.50-110.50
Qt. Water 44.50-55.50

Higgins & Seiter
Clarets 135.00-170.00
Wines 151.00-198.00

T. B. Clark & Co.
HENRY VIII
Qt. Tankard Jug
Each 99.00-115.00

T. B. Clark & Co.
WINOLA
Qt. Jug
Each 88.00-99.00

T. B. Clark & Co.
ADONIS
Flemish Jug
Each 250.00-275.00

T. B. Clark & Co.
VENUS
Whiskey Flagon
Each 175.00-225.00

T. B. Clark & Co.
VENUS
Wide Mouth Jug
Pt. 154.00-162.00
Qt. 162.00-181.00
3 Pt. 187.00-209.00

T. B. Clark & Co.
DESDEMONA
Priscilla Jug
Each 302.00-331.00

Higgins & Seiter
MANILLA
Whiskey Jug
Each 99.00-121.00

T. B. Clark & Co.
WINOLA
Wide Mouth Jug
½ Pt. 71.50-82.50
Pt. 82.50-93.50
Qt. 104.50-126.50
3 Pt. 126.50-137.50
½ Gal. 137.50-165.50

DECANTERS and JUGS

T. B. Clark & Co.
STRAW & FAN
Qt. w/handle .142.00-157.00
W/O handle ..115.00-142.00

T. B. Clark & Co.
WINOLA
Quart handled
Each 102.00-134.00

J. D. Bergen
SAVOY
3 Pt. 250.00-300.00

J. D. Bergen
ELECTRIC
Pt. 115.00-121.00

Pitkins & Brooks
DELMAR
P & B Grade
Each 165.00-190.00

Averbeck
LIBERTY
Each 157.00-190.00

J. D. Bergen
GLENWOOD
1 Qt. 152.00-184.00

DECANTERS and JUGS

Higgins & Seiter
CLARET JUG
Qt. 94.00-105.00
Qt. Claret 110.00-121.00
Pt. 79.00-94.00
Pt. Claret 89.00-105.00

T. B. Clark & Co.
WINOLA
Qt. - No Handle
Each 92.00-111.00

Averbeck
FLORIDA
Pt. 105.00-110.00
Qt. 115.00-131.00

Higgins & Seiter
FLORENTINE
Whiskey Decanter
Pt. 79.00-126.00
Qt. 89.00-94.00
Claret
Pt. 89.00-94.00
Qt. 94.00-115.00
Whiskey Tumbler
Doz. 105.00-126.00

T. B. Clark & Co.
PALMETTO
½ Gal. 136.00-205.00

Higgins & Seiter
NAPOLEON
Each 110.00-157.00

T. B. Clark & Co.
PALMETTO
Qt. 121.00-152.00
3 Pt. 161.00-199.00

Averbeck
ALABAMA
Pt. 102.00-131.00
Qt. 136.00-163.00

Averbeck
FLORIDA
No Handle
Pt. 94.00-121.00

Higgins & Seiter
GEORGIA
13" 94.00-121.00

Higgins & Seiter
CUT STAR
Qt. Claret 147.00-157.00
Pt. Claret 168.00-178.00

DECANTERS and JUGS

Higgins & Seiter
STRAWBERRY
DIAMOND FAN
Each 190.00-220.00

T. B. Clark & Co.
ARBUTUS
with Sterling Top
Each 190.00-235.00

T. B. Clark & Co.
CORAL
No Handle 157.00-173.00
Handle 178.00-189.00

T. B. Clark & Co.
MANHATTAN
No Handle 131.00-142.00
Handle 142.00-152.00

Pitkins & Brooks
ORIOLE
P & B Grade
Qt. 155.00-200.00

Pitkins & Brooks
SUNRAY
P & B Grade
1½ Pt. 176.00-197.00

T. B. Clark & Co.
PALMETTO
Fleming Jugs
Each 100.00-185.00
depending on size

T. B. Clark & Co.
DESDEMONA
Jug 150.00-200.00

T. B. Clark & Co.
ARBUTUS
Wide Mouth Jug
½ Pt. 90.00-110.00
Pt. 120.00-160.00
Qt. 135.00-160.00
3 Pt. 160.00-190.00
½ Gal. 190.00-220.00

Higgins & Seiter
CUT STAR
Each 47.00-89.00

Pitkins & Brooks
AURORA BOREALIS
P & B Grade
1½ Pt. 250.00-300.00

T. B. Clark & Co.
MANHATTAN
½ Pt. 52.00-63.00
Pt. 68.00-79.00
Qt. 84.00-100.00
3 Pt. 126.00-136.00
½ Gal. 131.00-147.00

FINGER BOWLS

J. D. Bergen
GOLF
4½" 27.00-34.00
5" 34.00-40.00

Averbeck
OCCIDENT
Each 38.00-44.00

Averbeck
GEORGIA
Each 34.00-40.00

J. D. Bergen
ELECTRIC
4½" 27.00-34.00
5" 34.00-40.00

Pitkins & Brooks
MARS
P & B Grade
Each 44.00-50.00

Pitkins & Brooks
RAJAH
P & B Grade
Each 55.00-61.00

Pitkins & Brooks
STANDARD
Each 34.00-40.00

Pitkins & Brooks
Standard Grade
Each 23.00-29.00

Pitkins & Brooks
BELMONT
P & B Grade
Each 61.00-65.00

Pitkins & Brooks
IMPORTED
Each 23.00-29.00

Pitkins & Brooks
BELMONT
P & B Grade
Each 60.00-65.00

Higgins & Seiter
STRAWBERRY
DIAMOND FAN
Each 39.00-44.00

J. D. Bergen
PREMIER
4½" 28.00-34.00
5" 39.00-44.00

Higgins & Seiter
NAPOLEON
Each 23.00-29.00

Higgins & Seiter
FLORENCE
Each 29.00-34.00

T. B. Clark & Co.
P.E.
Each 29.00-34.00

T. B. Clark & Co.
WINOLA
Each 29.00-34.00

Higgins & Seiter
Each 29.00-39.00

Higgins & Seiter
CUT STAR
Each 34.00-40.00

Higgins & Seiter
SPECIAL FLORENTINE
Each 27.00-34.00

T. B. Clark & Co.
WINOLA
Each 47.00-58.00

GOBLETS

Pitkins & Brooks
26.00-37.00

Averbeck
FLORIDA
60.00-65.00

Pitkins & Brooks
SUNRISE
19.00-26.00

Higgins & Seiter
CUT STAR
26.00-37.00

Pitkins & Brooks
BELMONT
P & B Grade
80.00-90.00

Averbeck
VIENNA
55.00-75.00

Pitkins & Brooks
HEART
P & B Grade
80.00-100.00

Higgins & Seiter
FLORENCE
47.00-55.00

Pitkins & Brooks
MERLIN
55.00-75.00

Higgins & Seiter
STRAWBERRY
DIAMOND FAN
40.00-45.00

Pitkins & Brooks
Standard Grade
40.00-50.00

J. D. Bergen
PREMIER
40.00-50.00

Averbeck
ALABAMA
47.00-63.00

Pitkins & Brooks
Standard Grade
40.00-44.00

Higgins & Seiter
DEWEY
19.00-26.00

Averbeck
FLORIDA
55.00-75.00

J. D. Bergen
ELECTRIC
55.00-75.00

J. D. Bergen
ELECTRIC
55.00-75.00

J. D. Bergen
GOLF
55.00-75.00

Pitkins & Brooks
50.00-63.00

Pitkins & Brooks
42.00-50.00

J. D. Bergen
MARIE
55.00-75.00

Higgins & Seiter
FLORENTINE
47.00-55.00

J. D. Bergen
MARIE
73.00-89.00

Higgins & Seiter
47.00-55.00

Averbeck
LIBERTY
47.00-55.00

Averbeck
NAPLES
47.00-55.00

GOBLETS

J. D. Bergen
ELECTRIC
45.00-60.00

J. D. Bergen
GOLF
45.00-60.00

J. D. Bergen
PREMIER
80.00-95.00

J. D. Bergen
GOLF
45.00-60.00

J. D. Bergen
PREMIER
80.00-95.00

Pitkins & Brooks
VENICE
34.00-45.00

Averbeck
ALABAMA
45.00-60.00

J. D. Bergen
MARIE
45.00-60.00

Averbeck
FLORIDA
45.00-60.00

J. D. Bergen
PREMIER
45.00-60.00

J. D. Bergen
ELECTRIC
34.00-50.00

Pitkins & Brooks
SUNRISE
12.00-15.00

J. D. Bergen
ELECTRIC
42.00-47.00

J. D. Bergen
PREMIER
42.00-47.00

Pitkins & Brooks
HEART
P & B Grade
110.00-125.00

Averbeck
RADIUM
42.00-47.00

J. D. Bergen
ELECTRIC
42.00-47.00

Pitkins & Brooks
42.00-47.00

Pitkins & Brooks
37.00-42.00

Pitkins & Brooks
37.00-42.00

Pitkins & Brooks
37.00-42.00

Averbeck
FLORIDA
44.00-60.00

Pitkins & Brooks
Standard Grade
37.00-42.00

Averbeck
ALABAMA
42.00-47.00

Averbeck
PRISCILLA
44.00-60.00

GOBLETS

Averbeck
FLORIDA
42.00-47.00

J. D. Bergen
GOLF
31.00-42.00

Averbeck
FLORIDA
42.00-47.00

Averbeck
ALABAMA
29.00-34.00

J. D. Bergen
ELECTRIC
29.00-34.00

Pitkins & Brooks
VENICE
29.00-50.00

Pitkins & Brooks
SUNRISE
10.00-16.00

Pitkins &.Brooks
P & B Grade
100.00-125.00

J. D. Bergen
GOLF
47.00-60.00

Averbeck
FLORIDA
34.00-40.00

J. D. Bergen
PREMIER
40.00-45.00

Averbeck
RUBY
45.00-50.00

Averbeck
GEORGIA
40.00-44.00

T. B. Clark & Co.
WINOLA
29.00-34.00

T. B. Clark & Co.
WINOLA
29.00-42.00

J. D. Bergen
ELECTRIC
38.00-47.00

J. D. Bergen
MARIE
47.00-60.00

Averbeck
ALABAMA
40.00-47.00

Pitkins & Brooks
BELMONT
P & B Grade
57.00-75.00

Pitkins & Brooks
57.00-75.00

Pitkins & Brooks
39.00-45.00

Pitkins & Brooks
45.00-61.00

Pitkins & Brooks
39.00-50.00

Pitkins & Brook
23.00-29.00

ICE CREAM

Pitkins & Brooks
ICE CREAM TRAY
Standard Grade
15" 407.50-457.50

Pitkins & Brooks
MERLIN
Footed Sherbet
Each 105.00-135.00

Pitkins & Brooks
ICE CREAM SAUCER
Standard Grade
6" 65.00-75.00

J. D. Bergen
MILDRED
Footed Sherbet
Each 55.00-70.00

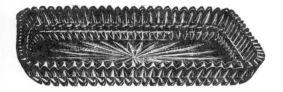

Averbeck
RENAISSANCE
Ice Cream Tray
8"x12" 70.00-75.00

Higgins & Seiter
WEBSTER
Ice Cream Saucer
5" or 6" 45.00-50.00

Higgins & Seiter
WASHINGTON
Ice Cream Saucer
6" 40.00-50.00

Pitkins & Brooks
OAK LEAF
Ice Cream Saucer
P & B Grade
6" 70.00-85.00

Pitkins & Brooks
OAK LEAF
Ice Cream Tray
P & B Grade
13" 361.50-501.50

ICE CREAM TRAYS

Averbeck
RUBY
Ice Cream Tray
14'' 255.00-270.00

Averbeck
VIENNA
Ice Cream Tray
14'' 255.00-270.00

Averbeck
FRISCO
Ice Cream Tray
14'' 255.00-270.00

T. B. Clark & Co.
WINOLA
Ice Cream Tray
Each 295.00-355.00

T. B. Clark & Co.
VENUS
Ice Cream Tray
Each 315.00-355.00

T. B. Clark & Co.
ADONIS
Ice Cream Tray
Each 315.00-365.00

T. B. Clark & Co.
MANHATTAN
Ice Cream Tray
Each 350.00-395.00

ICE CREAM TRAYS

Higgins & Seiter
ARLINGTON
Ice Cream Tray
8½''x13½'' 225.00-265.00

Higgins & Seiter
WEBSTER
Ice Cream Tray
14''x8½'' 240.00-280.00

J. D. Bergen
PROGRESS
Ice Cream Tray
18''x10½'' 355.00-430.00
14''x8'' 280.00-355.00

J. D. Bergen
FRISCO
Ice Cream Tray
10½''x18'' 355.00-415.00

J. D. Bergen
SEYMOUR
10''x16'' 375.00-440.00

J. D. Bergen
KENWOOD
9''x16'' 370.00-435.00

ICE CREAM TRAYS

J. D. Bergen
RAJAH
8''x14½'' 265.00-315.00

J. D. Bergen
ARABIAN
10''x16'' 315.00-365.00

AZALIA
9'' dia. 165.00-205.00
12'' dia. 225.00-260.00
14'' dia. 270.00-315.00

J. D. Bergen
PUTNAM
9''x16'' 465.00-515.00

J. D. Bergen
EAGLE
11''x17'' 365.00-415.00

ICE TUBS

J. D. Bergen
GLENWOOD
Plate and Drainer
6''x6½'' 190.00-205.00

J. D. Bergen
FLORIDA
Tub and Plate
5¾''x7¾'' 180.00-195.00

J. D. Bergen
GOLF
7'' 150.00-160.00

Higgins & Seiter
BELVEDERE
Footed
5''x9'' 131.00-152.00

J. D. Bergen
AMAZON
4¾''x7'' 200.00-210.00

Higgins & Seiter
ADMIRAL
4''x6'' 155.00-160.00

J. D. Bergen
IVANHOE
Tub with Drainer
Each 150.00-185.00

T. B. Clark & Co.
CORAL
Tub and Plate
Each 200.00-247.00

Higgins & Seiter
THE ESTELLE
4¾''x4'' 105.00-115.00

Higgins & Seiter
NAPOLEON
Tub and Plate
Each 126.00-142.00

Higgins & Seiter
WEBSTER
4''x4½'' 126.00-131.00

Higgins & Seiter
ARLINGTON
Tub with Drainer
7''x4¼'' 94.50-115.50

ICE TUBS

T. B. Clark & Co.
JEWEL
Each 145.00-160.00

Averbeck
IVY
10''x5'' 115.00-147.00

Averbeck
RADIUM
3¾'' high 115.00-126.00

Averbeck
MAUD ADAMS
6''x9'' 110.00-150.00

MISCELLANEOUS BOWLS

Pitkins & Brooks
SPARKLE
Nut Bowl
Standard Grade
6'' 63.00-84.00

Pitkins & Brooks
AERO
Nut Bowl
P & B Grade
5½'' 63.00-79.00

Pitkins & Brooks
ST. REGIS
Nut Bowl
P & B Grade
5½'' 63.00-79.00

Pitkins & Brooks
STAR
Whipped Cream
Standard Grade
7'' 79.00-105.00

Averbeck
LIBERTY
Whipped Cream
7''x4½'' 125.00-150.00

Pitkins & Brooks
SAVANNAH MELON
P & B Grade
7½'' 115.00-131.00

JEWEL BOXES and HAIR RECEIVERS

Pitkins & Brooks
DELMAR
Jewel Box
P & B Grade
7'' 90.00-110.00

Pitkins & Brooks
HIAWATHA
Jewel Box
P & B Grade
Each 75.00-90.00

Pitkins & Brooks
MERRIMAC
Jewel Box
P & B Grade
6'' 75.00-90.00

Pitkins & Brooks
SPARKLE
Jewel Box
P & B Grade
7'' 90.00-125.00

J. D. Bergen
OAKLAND
Jewel Case
3½''x4'' 75.00-90.00

Pitkins & Brooks
ELECTRA
Hair Receiver
Each 50.00-75.00

Pitkins & Brooks
AURORA BOREALIS
Hair Receiver
P & B Grade
5'' 75.00-110.00

Pitkins & Brooks
HIAWATHA
Hair Receiver
P & B Grade
5'' 50.00-75.00

Pitkins & Brooks
ALLADIN
Hair Receiver
P & B Grade
4½'' 50.00-75.00

Pitkins & Brooks
LAROSE
Hair Receiver
P & B Grade
5'' 50.00-75.00

Pitkins & Brooks
ESTHER
Hair Receiver
P & B Grade
5'' 41.00-49.00

Pitkins & Brooks
ASTER
Hair Receiver
Standard Grade
5'' 41.00-58.00

LAMPS

Pitkins & Brooks
CHRYSANTHEMUM
Electric Lamp, Engraved
P & B Grade
with 32 Prisms
17" 1,070.00

Pitkins & Brooks
DELMAR
Electric Lamp
Rock Crystal Effect
P & B Grade
with or without prisms
17" 1,070.00

Pitkins & Brooks
POPPY
Electric Lamp, Engraved
P & B Grade
with Prisms
22" 1,070.00

Pitkins & Brooks
ARC
Electric Lamp and Shade
P & B Grade
12½" 577.50

Higgins & Seiter
CRYSANTHEMUM
23" 1,030.00

Higgins & Seiter
RICH CUT GLASS
21" 1,015.00

Pitkins & Brooks
ELECTRA
Electric Lamp
P & B Grade
26'' 1,370.00

Pitkins & Brooks
ORO
Electric Lamp and Shade
P & B Grade
14'' 1,010.00

Pitkins & Brooks
AURORA BOREALIS
Electric Lamp
P & B Grade
12½''x6'' 470.00

Pitkins & Brooks
DELMAR
Electric
P & B Grade
with Prisms
14'' 595.00

LAMPS

J. D. Bergen
KENWOOD
Silver Plated Mountings
and Fount
22'' 1,220.00

J. D. Bergen
PREMIER
14½'' 1,010.00
22'' 1,220.00

LAMPS

Pitkins & Brooks
DAISY
Electric Lamp, Engraved
P & B Grade
32 Prisms
17" 1,220.00

Pitkins & Brooks
PANSY
Electric Lamp, Engraved
P & B Grade
32 Prisms
17" 1,220.00

MISCELLANEOUS TABLE WARE

T. B. Clark & Co.
HENRY VIII
Sugar Sifter with
Sterling Top
Each 105.00-130.00

Pitkins & Brooks
TOPAZ
Grapefruit
P & B Grade
7½" across top 85.00-105.00

T. B. Clark & Co.
HENRY VIII
Tea Caddy with
Sterling Top
Each 95.00-115.00

Pitkins & Brooks
PRISM
Mayonnaise Bowl and
Plate
P & B Grade
6" 95.00-115.00

Averbeck
SARATOGA
Napkin Ring
Each 50.00-57.00

Pitkins & Brooks
OLIVE JAR
Imported
6½" 35.00-45.00

Pitkins & Brooks
BORDER NUT BOWL
P & B Grade
8" 179.00-183.00

T. B. Clark & Co.
HENRY VIII
Syrup Jug with
Plated Top
Small 115.00-140.00
Large 140.00-162.00

Pitkins & Brooks
PLAZA
Mayonnaise Boat
and Tray
P & B Grade
Pair 145.00-160.00

T. B. Clark & Co.
JEWEL
Pepper Sauce Bottle
Sterling Top
85.00-100.00

MISCELLANEOUS TABLE WARE

J. D. Bergen
GOLF
Horse Radish
6".........55.00-63.00

Higgins & Seiter
HORSE RADISH JAR
H & S
5¼"........55.00-63.00

J. D. Bergen
SAVOY
Horse Radish Jar
Each........55.00-63.00

Higgins & Seiter
NAPOLEON
Horse Radish Jar
5¼"........53.00-59.00

J. D. Bergen
ELECTRIC
Horse Radish Jar
Each........53.00-70.00

Higgins & Seiter
RENAISSANCE
Horse Radish Jar
5¼"........33.00-37.00

Pitkins & Brooks
DELMAR
Worcestershire Bottle
P & B Grade
8".........52.50-62.50

Pitkins & Brooks
IMPORTED HORSE
RADISH
Each........30.00-35.00

STRAWBERR
& FAN
Worcestershire
Bottle
8".......22.50-27.50

Higgins & Seiter
STRAWBERRY
& FAN
Horse Radish Jar
5¼"............30.00-33.00

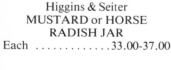

Higgins & Seiter
MUSTARD or HORSE
RADISH JAR
Each.............33.00-37.00

Higgins & Seiter
NAPOLEON
Mustard or Horse
Radish Jar
Each.............30.00-47.00

Higgins & Seiter
RENAISSANCE
Mustard or Horse
Radish Jar
Each.............30.00-37.00

Higgins & Seiter
STRAWBERRY
DIAMOND & FAN
Catsup Bottle
7"...............33.00-37.00

Higgins & Seiter
STRAWBERRY
DIAMOND & FAN
Tabasco Sauce Bottle
Each.............33.00-37.00

Pitkins & Brooks
DELMAR
Tabasco Sauce Bottle
P & B Grade
Each.............33.00-40.00

Higgins & Seiter
MAJESTIC
Worcestershire Bottle
Each.............33.00-42.00

Higgins & Seiter
7"...............33.00-40.00

MISCELLANEOUS

Higgins & Seiter
Cigar Cutter and Ash
Receiver - cut glass
and sterling silver
4'' 55.00-75.00

Pitkins & Brooks
HIAWATHA FERN
Dish and Liner
P & B Grade
8'' 130.00-135.00

Pitkins & Brooks
TOPAZ
Clock
P & B Grade
5½'' 230.00-355.00

Averbeck
PRISM
Loving Cup
½ Pt. 40.00-60.00

Pitkins & Brooks
MURONO
Ash Tray
P & B Grade
3½''-5½'' . . .35.00-50.00

Pitkins & Brooks
CURIO DISH
P & B Grade
9'' 90.00-115.00

Averbeck
PAPER WEIGHT
Each 42.50

Averbeck
LONDON
Oval Bowl or Dish
12'' 95.00-115.00

J. D. Bergen
GIRARD
Fancy Tray or Cake Plate
6½''x14'' 330.00-377.00

Pitkins & Brooks
DON
Card Case
P & B Grade
4'' 27.50-32.50

Pitkins & Brooks
VIVIAN
Hat Pin Holder
P & B Grade
7'' 45.00-60.00

J. D. Bergen
MADONNA
Cake or Bread Tray
11½''x7'' 83.00-100.00

PICKLE DISHES and OLIVE TRAYS

Averbeck
MARIETTA
Pickle Dish
8'' 53.00-57.00

Averbeck
SARATOGA
Pickle Dish
8'' 62.00-70.00

Averbeck
RUBY
Pickle Dish
8'' 70.00-77.00

Averbeck
ROYAL
Pickle Dish
8'' 62.00-67.00

Averbeck
CANTON
Pickle Dish
8'' 62.00-67.00

Averbeck
EMPRESS
Pickle Dish
8'' 67.00-77.00

Averbeck
SARATOGA
Olive Dish
7¼'' 50.00-60.00

Averbeck
MARIETTA
Olive Dish
7¾'' 50.00-60.00

Averbeck
LADY CURZON
Olive Dish
7¾'' 50.00-60.00

Pitkins & Brooks
NELLORE
Pickle Dish
P & B Grade
7'' 62.00-72.00

Averbeck
CANTON
7¾'' 50.00-60.00

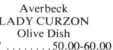

Pitkins & Brooks
MEADVILLE
Pickle Dish
Standard Grade
7'' 50.00-55.00

Averbeck
RUBY
Olive Dish
7¾'' 43.00-47.00

Averbeck
PRISCILLA
Olive Dish
7¾'' 43.00-47.00

PITCHERS and TANKARDS

Averbeck
FLORIDA
2 Pint Water
10½" 155.00-195.00

Averbeck
NAPLES
4 Pint Water
10½" 195.00-230.00

Averbeck
GEORGIA
3 Pint Jug
9¾"x7½" 165.00-185.00

J. D. Bergen
GOLDENROD
2 Quart Pitcher
Each 185.00-230.00

Higgins & Seiter
LAKELAND
Claret Pitcher
Sterling Silver Mounted
1 Qt. 100.00-130.00
3 Pts. 200.00-230.00

J. D. Bergen
DELTA
½ Pt. 90.00-105.00
1 Pt. 110.00-125.00
1 Qt. 130.00-165.00
2 Qt. 165.00-185.00

PITCHERS and TANKARDS

Higgins & Seiter
SYROTT
Claret Pitcher
1 Qt. 135.00-162.00
3 Pts. 162.00-190.00

Averbeck
NICE
2 Pt. 205.00-255.00

Higgins & Seiter
MAINE
Claret Pitcher
1 Qt. 95.00-130.00
2 Pts. 135.00-180.00

Higgins & Seiter
NAPOLEON
1 Pt. 92.00-110.00
1 Qt. 110.00-127.00
2 Pts. 127.00-162.00

Higgins & Seiter
STRAWBERRY
DIAMOND FAN
1/3 Pt. 85.00-95.00
1/2 Pt. 95.00-110.00
1 Pt. 110.00-120.00
1 Qt. 120.00-135.00
3 Pts. 135.00-150.00

Higgins & Seiter
STRAWBERRY
DIAMOND FAN
Tankard Jug
½ Pt. 72.50-92.50
1 Pt. 82.50-92.50
1 Qt. 87.50-102.50
3 Pts. 97.50-112.50
2 Qts. 112.50-127.50

Higgins & Seiter
LAKELAND
Claret Jug
11" 155.00-205.00

Higgins & Seiter
STRAWBERRY
DIAMOND FAN
Tankard Jug
1 Qt. 37.50-47.50
2½ Pts. 52.50-67.50
3 Pts. 72.50-82.50
2 Qts. 82.50-97.50

PITCHERS and TANKARDS

Pitkins & Brooks
STANDARD
Jug
3 Pts. 105.00-130.00

J. D. Bergen
ALLYN
1 Qt. 155.00-165.00
2 Qt. 185.00-215.00

Averbeck
RUBY
2 Pt. 93.50-123.50

J. D. Bergen
GOLF
Claret
2 Qt. 260.00-280.00

J. D. Bergen
PERSIAN
Claret Jug
3 Pt. 205.00-230.00

Pitkins & Brooks
ORLEANS
Jug
P & B Grade
4 Pt. 180.00-183.00

J. D. Bergen
PREMIER
Claret Jug
2 Qt. 345.00-380.00

PITCHERS and TANKARDS

Averbeck
GENOA
Water
3 Pt. 162.50-182.50

J. D. Bergen
IVY
Claret Jug
3 Pt. 255.00-305.00

J. D. Bergen
ELECTRIC
Claret Jug
2 Qt. 315.00-340.00

Averbeck
VIENNA
3 Pt. 135.00-160.00

J. D. Bergen
PRINCETON
Claret Jug
3 Pts. 305.00-330.00

Averbeck
TRIXY
2 Pt. 95.00-120.00
3 Pt. 130.00-155.00

PITCHERS and TANKARDS

Averbeck
FLORIDA
2 Pt. 115.00-130.00
3 Pt. 125.00-150.00

J. D. Bergen
PREMIER
Claret Jug
3 Pt. 262.50-317.50

Averbeck
SARATOGA
4 Pt. 157.00-170.00

Averbeck
VIENNA
2 Pt. 85.00-117.00
3 Pt. 117.00-150.00

Averbeck
GENOA
4 Pt. 262.50-192.50

Averbeck
ALABAMA
2 Pt. 130.00-140.00
3 Pt. 162.00-192.00

Pitkins & Brooks
KELZ JUG
Standard Grade
3 Pt. 92.00-105.00

Averbeck
MAUD ADAMS
4 Pt. 155.00-180.00

PITCHERS and TANKARDS

J. D. Bergen
BEDFORD
1 Qt. 145.00-175.00
2 Qt. 180.00-215.00

J. D. Bergen
ETHEL
1 Qt. 155.00-182.00
2 Qt. 200.00-230.00

J. D. Bergen
DALLAS
2 Qt. 305.00-320.00

J. D. Bergen
GOLF
½ Pt. 92.50-102.50
1 Pt. 107.50-122.50
1 Qt. 147.50-167.50
2 Qt. 182.50-207.50

Averbeck
VIENNA
3 Pt. 120.00-150.00

Higgins & Seiter
AMAZON
Cut Glass with Sterling Silver
hand-chased mounting
2 Pt. 97.00-110.00
3 Pt. 110.00-122.00

Averbeck
GEORGIA
1 Pt. 85.00-110.00

PITCHERS and TANKARDS

J. D. Bergen
MARIE
2 Qt. 240.00-250.00

J. D. Bergen
COLONY
2 Qt. 240.00-255.00

J. D. Bergen
PREMIER
1 Qt. 162.50-192.50
2 Qt. 192.50-210.50

J. D. Bergen
EVANS
1 Qt. 110.00-155.00
2 Qt. 155.00-195.00

Higgins & Seiter
OTIS
2 Qt. 115.00-140.00
1 Qt. 85.00-110.00

Higgins & Seiter
DEWEY
2 Qt. 125.00-150.00
1 Qt. 100.00-125.00

Averbeck
RUBY
2 Pt. 100.00-125.00
3 Pt. 130.00-155.00

PITCHERS and TANKARDS

J. D. Bergen
GOLF
1 Pt. 105.00-133.00
2 Qt. 133.00-150.00

J. D. Bergen
WILLARD
1 Qt. 155.00-205.00
2 Qt. 182.00-235.00

J. D. Bergen
FEDERAL
2 Qt. 227.00-255.00

Averbeck
RUBY
3 Pt. 142.00-180.00

Pitkins & Brooks
ORLEANS JUG
P & B Grade
3 Pt. 115.00-140.00

PLATEAUS

Pitkins & Brooks
MOUNTED PLATEAU
Silver Plated
Standard Grade
10" 60.00-75.00
12" 95.00-105.00
14" 105.00-115.00
16" 115.00-135.00
18" 135.00-155.00

Pitkins & Brooks
MOUNTED PLATEAU
Silver Plated
Standard Grade
10" 50.00-60.00
12" 65.00-75.00
14" 75.00-85.00
16" 85.00-100.00
18" 100.00-117.00

Pitkins & Brooks
HANDLED TRAY
Silver Plated
Standard Grade
12" 55.00-65.00
14" 65.00-75.00
16" 85.00-100.00

Pitkins & Brooks
MOUNTED PLATEAU
Silver Plated
Standard Grade
8" 30.00-42.00
10" 47.00-62.00
12" 57.00-72.00
14" 67.00-92.00

Pitkins & Brooks
MOUNTED PLATEAU
Silver Plated
Standard Grade
10" 37.00-47.00
12" 47.00-57.00
14" 62.00-77.00

Pitkins & Brooks
MOUNTED PLATEAU
Silver Plated
Standard Grade
10" 37.00-52.00
12" 42.00-52.00
14" 52.00-67.00
16" 62.00-92.00

PLATEAUS

Pitkins & Brooks
BEADED PLATEAU
Standard Grade

8"	23.00-27.00
10"	27.00-37.00
12"	37.00-43.00
14"	43.00-47.00
16"	42.00-52.00
18"	55.00-70.00

Pitkins & Brooks
CONCAVE & BEADED
Standard Grade

8"	32.00-37.00
10"	37.00-47.00
12"	42.00-52.00
14"	52.00-65.00

Pitkins & Brooks
Standard Grade

10"	45.00-50.00
12"	50.00-55.00
14"	65.00-80.00
16"	80.00-105.00

Pitkins & Brooks
STAR PLATEAU
Standard Grade

8"	27.00-33.00
10"	33.00-37.00
12"	37.00-43.00
14"	43.00-47.00
16"	47.00-53.00
18"	53.00-63.00

Pitkins & Brooks
Standard Grade

10"	35.00-42.00
12"	42.00-47.00
16"	62.00-67.00
18"	67.00-80.00

PLATES and SAUCERS

Pitkins & Brooks
KENWOOD
SAUCER
5'' 55.00-71.00
6'' 71.00-77.00

Averbeck
BOSTON
7'' Plate 55.00-63.00

Averbeck
LOWELL
7'' Plate 44.00-55.00

J. D. Bergen
WEBSTER
Saucer
5'' 35.00-55.00
6'' 49.00-60.00

J. D. Bergen
BERMUDA
Saucer
5'' 46.00-57.00
6'' 66.00-71.00

Pitkins & Brooks
ROLAND
P & B Grade
9'' Plate . . .99.50-104.50
12'' Plate . .236.50-247.50
14'' Plate . .330.50-412.50

J. D. Bergen
MAGNET
Saucer
5'' 55.50-71.50
6'' 71.50-77.50

J. D. Bergen
CORSAIR
Saucer
5'' 46.00-49.00
6'' 52.00-64.00

Averbeck
VIENNA
7'' Plate 46.00-57.00

J. D. Bergen
GOLF
Saucer
5'' 35.00-49.00
6'' 49.00-57.00

PLATES and SAUCERS

J. D. Bergen
DELAWARE
9" 176.00-192.00

J. D. Bergen
LAWTON
Fancy Dish
4-Lobed . . .192.00-220.00

Averbeck
CAPE TOWN
Plate
7" 66.00-82.00

J. D. Bergen
ORIOLE
Fancy Dish
9" 231.00-258.00

Averbeck
NEWPORT
Plate
7" 66.00-82.00

J. D. Bergen
BEDFORD
Saucer
5" 49.50-60.50
6" 60.50-66.50

Averbeck
AMERICAN BEAUTY
Plate
7" 71.50-82.50

J. D. Bergen
ELECTRIC
Plate
7" 66.00-82.00

NAPPIES and SAUCERS

Pitkins & Brooks
BERRIE
Nappie
P & B Grade
8'' 136.00-168.00

T. B. Clark & Co.
DESDEMONA
7'' 121.00-131.00
8'' 136.00-152.00
9'' 163.00-173.00
10'' 178.00-199.00

T. B. Clark & Co.
VENUS
8'' 194.50-220.50
9'' 220.50-262.50

T. B. Clark & Co.
VENUS
7'' Round Plate
Each 42.00-52.00

Higgins & Seiter
JUBILEE
6'' 60.00-71.00

T. B. Clark & Co.
ADONIS
9'' 220.00-231.00

Averbeck
GEM
5'' 24.00-29.00

Higgins & Seiter
WEBSTER
6'' 37.00-47.00

Averbeck
SARATOGA
7'' Round Plate
Each 52.00-68.00

T. B. Clark & Co.
WINOLA
5'' 34.00-44.00
6'' 39.00-49.00
7'' 44.00-55.00

T. B. Clark & Co.
ARBUTUS
7'' 136.00-157.00
8'' 157.00-168.00
9'' 168.00-184.00
10'' 199.00-236.00

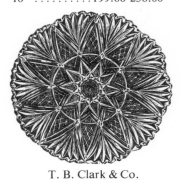

T. B. Clark & Co.
MANHATTAN
5'' 26.00-29.00
6'' 29.00-31.00
7'' 34.00-50.00

Pitkins & Brooks
BEAVER SAUCER
Standard Grade
5'' 26.00-37.00
6'' 37.00-47.00

NAPPIES

Pitkins & Brooks
MIKADO HANDLED
Standard Grade
5'' 47.00-52.00
6'' 58.00-68.00

Pitkins & Brooks
MEADVILLE
Standard Grade
5'' 26.00-31.00
6'' 31.00-37.00

Pitkins & Brooks
VENICE
P & B Grade
5'' 37.00-42.00
6'' 42.00-47.00

Pitkins & Brooks
MARS
P & B Grade
5'' 42.00-52.00
6'' 52.00-68.00

Averbeck
DIAMOND
with handle:
5'' 63.00-73.00
6'' 73.00-89.00
without handle:
5'' 58.00-68.00
6'' 79.00-89.00

Averbeck
FRISCO
6'' 52.00-68.00

Averbeck
DIANA
with handle:
5'' 63.00-73.00
6'' 73.00-89.00
without handle:
5'' 63.00-73.00
6'' 73.00-89.00

Averbeck
MARIETTA
with handle:
5'' 34.00-44.00
6'' 44.00-55.00
without handle:
5'' 31.00-42.00
6'' 42.00-52.00

Averbeck
VIENNA
with handle:
5'' 31.00-37.00
6'' 37.00-47.00
without handle:
5'' 31.00-37.00
6'' 37.00-47.00

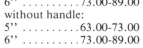

NAPPIES

J. D. Bergen
EMBLEM
5" Hdl 52.00-63.00
6" Hdl 73.00-84.00

J. D. Bergen
PROGRESS
5" 63.00-73.00
6" 79.00-89.00

J. D. Bergen
CORSAIR
5" Hdl 37.00-47.00
6" Hdl 52.00-63.00

J. D. Bergen
WEBSTER
5" Hdl 52.00-79.00
6" Hdl 73.00-84.00

J. D. Bergen
BEDFORD
5" Hdl 52.00-68.00
6" Hdl 68.00-84.00

J. D. Bergen
BERMUDA
5" Hdl 42.00-49.00
6" Hdl 49.00-60.00

Pitkins & Brooks
MYRTLE BERRY
Standard Grade
7" 31.00-34.00
8" 47.00-60.00

Pitkins & Brooks
CORSAIR BERRY
Standard Grade
7" 52.00-58.00
8" 63.00-73.00
9" 73.00-94.00

Pitkins & Brooks
MEADVILLE BERRY
Standard Grade
7" 42.00-47.00
8" 47.00-58.00
9" 63.00-79.00

NAPPIES

J. D. Bergen
GOLF
5" Hdl 52.00-63.00
6" Hdl 63.00-79.00

J. D. Bergen
WEBSTER
5" Hdl 52.00-63.00
6" Hdl 63.00-68.00

Pitkins & Brooks
MIKADO
Berry
Standard Grade
7" 63.00-79.00

Averbeck
CAPE TOWN
7" 110.00-126.00
8" 126.00-136.00
9" 157.00-199.00
10" 168.00-199.00

Averbeck
CANTON
7" 52.00-63.00
8" 68.00-81.00
9" 81.00-102.00
10" 105.00-126.00

Averbeck
REGAL
7" 52.00-63.00
8" 73.00-84.00
9" 84.00-105.00
10" 110.00-126.00

Averbeck
RUBY
without handle:
5" 26.00-47.00
6" 47.00-58.00
with handle:
5" 63.00-68.00
6" 73.00-79.00

Averbeck
NAPLES
without handle:
5" 52.00-79.00
6" 79.00-89.00
with handle:
5" 89.00-100.00
6" 100.00-115.00

Averbeck
CANTON
without handle:
5" 31.00-47.00
6" 47.00-58.00
with handle:
5" 63.00-68.00
6" 73.00-79.00

Averbeck
LADY CURZON
without handle:
5" 31.00-47.00
6" 47.00-58.00
with handle:
5" 63.00-68.00
6" 73.00-78.00

NAPPIES

J. D. Bergen
AMBROSE
7" 115.00-142.00
8" 142.00-173.00
9" 157.00-189.00
10" 168.00-199.00

J. D. Bergen
CORSAIR
7" 63.00-84.00
8" 84.00-94.00
9" 115.00-141.00
10" 147.00-199.00

J. D. Bergen
KENWOOD
7" 105.00-115.00
8" 142.00-157.00
9" 157.00-197.00

J. D. Bergen
BEDFORD
7" 73.00-84.00
8" 84.00-100.00
9" 100.00-131.00
10" 136.00-157.00

NAPPIES

Averbeck
RUBY
7" 58.00-68.00
8" 68.00-79.00
9" 84.00-94.00
10" 115.00-131.00

Averbeck
MARIETTA
7" 73.00-84.00
8" 84.00-94.00
9" 94.00-115.00
10" 126.00-157.00

Averbeck
OCCIDENT
7" 136.00-162.00
8" 152.00-173.00
9" 199.00-225.00
10" 231.00-262.00

Averbeck
PUCK
7" 63.00-73.00
8" 73.00-84.00
9" 99.00-105.00
10" 105.00-136.00

Averbeck
PARIS
7" 63.00-70.00
8" 71.00-94.00
9" 99.00-118.00
10" 131.00-165.00

Averbeck
FRISCO
7" 58.00-68.00
8" 68.00-84.00
9" 89.00-115.00
10" 131.00-165.00

Averbeck
SARATOGA
7" 68.00-75.00
8" 75.00-91.00
9" 91.00-101.00
10" 118.00-157.00

Averbeck
BRUSSELS
7" 52.00-63.00
8" 63.00-78.00
9" 84.00-115.00
10" 115.00-131.00

Averbeck
SPRUCE
7" 52.00-63.00
8" 63.00-73.00
9" 73.00-89.00
10" 99.00-157.00

NAPPIES

Averbeck
ACME
7" 152.00-175.00
8" 175.00-186.00
9" 186.00-199.00
10" 204.00-236.00

Averbeck
NEWPORT
with handle:
5" 42.00-52.00
6" 47.00-57.00
without handle:
5" 26.00-31.00
6" 31.00-42.00

Averbeck
AMERICAN BEAUTY
7" 133.00-165.00
8" 165.00-189.00
9" 189.00-204.00
10" 204.00-220.00

Averbeck
AMERICAN BEAUTY
with handle:
5" 52.00-68.00
6" 73.00-84.00
without handle:
5" 31.00-42.00
6" 42.00-52.00

Averbeck
LIBERTY
with handle:
5" 52.00-68.00
6" 73.00-84.00
without handle:
5" 31.00-42.00
6" 42.00-52.00

Averbeck
SPRUCE
with handle:
5" 52.00-68.00
6" 73.00-84.00
without handle:
5" 31.00-42.00
6" 42.00-52.00

Averbeck
HUDSON
with handle:
5" 68.00-73.00
6" 78.00-89.00
without handle:
5" 47.00-52.00
6" 57.00-63.00

T. B. Clark & Co.
DESDEMONA
Each 165.00-186.00

Higgins & Seiter
ALASKA
5½" 26.00-31.00

T. B. Clark & Co.
JEWEL
7" 84.00-94.00
8" 105.00-120.00
9" 131.00-165.00
10" 178.00-199.00

T. B. Clark & Co.
JEWEL
5" 26.00-36.00
6" 42.00-52.00
7" 63.00-73.00

Higgins & Seiter
CLOVER
Leaf Shape
Each 26.00-29.00

T. B. Clark & Co.
MANHATTAN
7" 84.00-89.00
8" 94.00-115.00
9" 120.00-173.00
10" 178.00-199.00

NAPPIES

J. D. Bergen
ST. LOUIS
7'' 73.00-89.00
8'' 94.00-115.00
9'' 126.00-147.00
10'' 147.00-168.00

J. D. Bergen
KENWOOD
7'' 102.00-107.00
8'' 115.00-139.00
9'' 131.00-157.00
10'' 157.00-210.00

J. D. Bergen
GOLDENROD
7'' 68.00-84.00
8'' 94.00-110.00
9'' 115.00-147.00
10'' 152.00-173.00

J. D. Bergen
RENWICK
7'' 99.00-110.00
8'' 120.00-136.00
9'' 136.00-162.00
10'' 168.00-199.00

J. D. Bergen
BERMUDA
7'' 63.00-84.00
8'' 84.00-94.00
9'' 94.00-126.00
10'' 136.00-173.00

J. D. Bergen
GOLF
7'' 52.00-63.00
8'' 63.00-84.00
9'' 84.00-105.00
10'' 105.00-131.00

Pitkins & Brooks
ORIOLE HANDLED
Standard Grade
5'' 26.00-42.00
6'' 29.00-47.00

J. D. Bergen
HAMPTON
7'' 142.00-160.00
8'' 170.00-181.00
9'' 186.00-207.00
10'' 217.00-238.00

J. D. Bergen
WEBSTER
7'' 112.00-139.00
8'' 133.00-149.00
9'' 154.00-181.00
10'' 191.00-238.00

PUFF BOXES and GLOVE BOXES

Pitkins & Brooks
HEART PUFF BOX
P & B Grade
6" 68.00-84.00

Pitkins & Brooks
TECK PUFF BOX
P & B Grade
5¼" 50.00-61.00

Pitkins & Brooks
NORTHERN STAR
P & B Grade
6¾" 61.00-71.00

Pitkins & Brooks
ESTHER PUFF BOX
P & B Grade
5" 47.00-58.00

Pitkins & Brooks
ELECTRA PUFF BOX
P & B Grade
Each 47.00-58.00

Pitkins & Brooks
GRACE PUFF BOX
P & B Grade
3½" to 5½" 47.00-58.00

Pitkins & Brooks
MABELLE PUFF BOX
P & B Grade
Each 47.00-58.00

Pitkins & Brooks
ASTER PUFF BOX
Standard Grade
5" 47.00-58.00

Pitkins & Brooks
CRETE PUFF BOX
P & B Grade
Each 47.00-58.00

Pitkins & Brooks
DELMAR GLOBE BOX
P & B Grade
11" 236.00-283.00

Pitkins & Brooks
HIAWATHA
GLOVE BOX
P & B Grade
10½" 199.00-236.00

PUNCH BOWLS

Pitkins & Brooks
RAJAH
P & B Grade - footed
10" 367.00-420.00

Pitkins & Brooks
HEART
P & B Grade
12" 420.00-462.00
14" 462.00-525.00

Pitkins & Brooks
BEVERLY FOOTED
P & B Grade
12" 441.00-457.00
14" 472.00-509.00

J. D. Bergen
MARLOW
Low Footed
12" 441.00-499.00

PUNCH BOWLS

Pitkins & Brooks
CRETE
P & B Grade - footed
10'' 388.50-409.50
12'' 430.50-451.50

T. B. Clark & Co.
DESDEMONA
14'' 388.50-409.50

T. B. Clark & Co.
CORAL
12'' 420.00-462.00
14'' 459.00-480.00

T. B. Clark & Co.
ARBUTUS
14'' 462.00-499.00

Higgins & Seiter
WEBSTER
Each 420.00-459.00

J. D. Bergen
CORSAIR
14'' 512.00

PUNCH BOWLS

Pitkins & Brooks
SUNBURST
P & B Grade
12" 512.00-551.00

Pitkins & Brooks
CAROLYN
P & B Grade
14" 551.00-598.00

Pitkins & Brooks
CAROLYN
P & B Grade
12" 525.00-562.00

PUNCH BOWLS

Pitkins & Brooks
BELMONT
P & B Grade
14" 546.00-598.00

Pitkins & Brooks
GARLAND
P & B Grade
12" 525.00-556.00

Pitkins & Brooks
PLYMOUTH
P & B Grade
12" 409.00-451.00
14" 556.00-604.00

PUNCH BOWLS

J. D. Bergen
WABASH
14" 577.50-619.50

T. B. Clark & Co.
DESDEMONA
12" 341.00-386.00
14" 462.00-499.00

Higgins & Seiter
LEADER
14" 315.00-341.00

PUNCH BOWLS

J. D. Bergen
PEARL
14" 630.00-656.00

Higgins & Seiter
BEDFORD
14" 115.00-168.00

T. B. Clark & Co.
DESDEMONA
12" 315.00-331.00

PUNCH BOWLS

J. D. Bergen
ELGIN
14" 220.00-283.00

J. D. Bergen
ELSA
14" 220.00-278.00

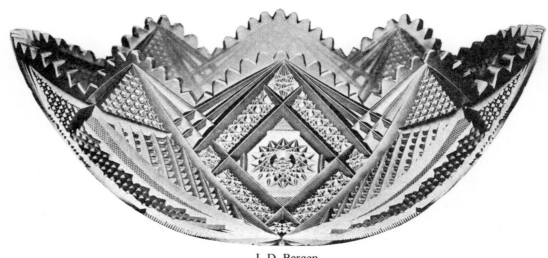

J. D. Bergen
ST. JAMES
15" 273.00-294.00

PUNCH BOWLS

Pitkins & Brooks
KEYSTONE
P & B Grade
10'' 136.00-189.00
12'' 241.00-325.00
14'' 325.00-409.00

J. D. Bergen
MONTICELLO
12'' 483.00-525.00
14'' 546.00-609.00

Pitkins & Brooks
SUNRAY
Standard Grade
12'' 210.00-294.00

Pitkins & Brooks
DERBY
P & B Grade
12'' 378.00-430.00
14'' 456.00-577.00

PUNCH BOWLS

Averbeck
VIENNA
10" 267.00-320.00
12" 341.00-383.00
14" 372.00-446.00

Averbeck
OCCIDENT
10" 483.00-535.00
12" 556.00-577.00
14" 693.00-745.00

J. D. Bergen
KENWOOD
12" 336.00-388.00
14" 483.00-525.00

J. D. Bergen
EDNA
14" 325.00-393.00

PUNCH BOWLS

J. D. Bergen
WABASH
Bowl 924.00
Cups ea. 46.00
Ladle 115.50
Plate 144.50
Set 2,310.00

PUNCH BOWLS

J. D. Bergen
PROGRESS
Bowl 1,039.00-1,270.00
Cup ea. 69.00
Set of cups (12) 981.00
Ladle 115.00
Plate 105.00
Set 3,255.00-4,042.00

J. D. Bergen
KENWOOD
Bowl 1,155.00-1,391.00
Cup ea. 75.00
Set of cups (12) 1,039.00
Ladle 115.00
Plate 105.00
Set 3,360.00-3,622.00

PUNCH BOWLS

J. D. Bergen
GOLF
12".................577.50-656.50
14".................656.50-721.50

Higgins & Seiter
NAPOLEON
14".................289.00-315.00

Higgins & Seiter
COMET
15".................488.00-525.00

PUNCH BOWLS

J. D. Bergen
KENWOOD

Bowl 1,039.50
Ladle .99.50
Cup w/plate ea. 57.50
Plateau 99.50
Set (with 12 cups) 2,887.50

SALT and PEPPER SHAKERS

Pitkins & Brooks
12.00-14.00

Pitkins & Brooks
12.00-14.00

Pitkins & Brooks
12.00-14.00

Pitkins & Brooks
14.00-18.00

Pitkins & Brooks
14.00-22.00

Pitkins & Brooks
Standard Grade
40.00-42.00

Pitkins & Brooks
Standard Grade
47.00-57.00

Pitkins & Brooks
Standard Grade
32.00-42.00

Pitkins & Brooks
20.00-22.00

Pitkins & Brooks
22.00-26.50

Pitkins & Brooks
25.50-29.00

J. D. Bergen
14.50-18.50

Pitkins & Brooks
32.50-38.50

Pitkins & Brooks
18.00-28.00

J. D. Bergen
26.50-36.00

J. D. Bergen
31.00-38.50

Pitkins & Brooks
Standard Grade
44.50-56.50

J. D. Bergen
18.00-24.00

J. D. Bergen
14.00-18.00

J. D. Bergen
22.00-29.00

J. D. Bergen
14.00-18.00

Pitkins & Brooks
27.00-37.00

J. D. Bergen
14.00-18.00

SALT and PEPPER SHAKERS

Pitkins & Brooks
25.00-30.00 pair

J. D. Bergen
14.00-21.00

Pitkins & Brooks
Standard Grade
32.00-42.00

Pitkins & Brooks
Standard Grade
27.00-32.00

J. D. Bergen
18.00-24.00

J. D. Bergen
20.00-26.00

Pitkins & Brooks
19.00-24.00

Pitkins & Brooks
19.00-24.00

J. D. Bergen
14.00-21.00

J. D. Bergen
18.00-24.00

J. D. Bergen
14.00-21.00

Pitkins & Brooks
21.00-26.00

Pitkins & Brooks
14.00-21.00

Pitkins & Brooks
32.00-42.00

Pitkins & Brooks
14.00-18.00

J. D. Bergen
32.00-38.00

Pitkins & Brooks
21.00-26.00

J. D. Bergen
36.00-44.00

Pitkins & Brooks
12.00-18.00

Pitkins & Brooks
28.00-36.00

SALT and PEPPER SHAKERS

J. D. Bergen
10.00-15.00

Pitkins & Brooks
Standard Grade
27.00-32.00

J. D. Bergen
14.00-19.00

J. D. Bergen
21.00-26.00

J. D. Bergen
21.00-26.00

Pitkins & Brooks
12.00-18.00

Pitkins & Brooks
12.00-14.00

T. B. Clark & Co.
HENRY VIII
50.00-65.00

Pitkins & Brooks
Standard Grade
21.00-26.00

Pitkins & Brooks
Standard Grade
21.00-26.00

Pitkins & Brooks
12.00-16.00

Higgins & Seiter
35.00-50.00

Pitkins & Brooks
30.00-40.00

Higgins & Seiter
35.00-42.00

Pitkins & Brooks
Standard Grade
30.00-37.00

Higgins & Seiter
30.00-32.00

Pitkins & Brooks
Standard Grade
30.00-35.00

Pitkins & Brooks
Standard Grade
32.00-40.00

Pitkins & Brooks
12.00-18.00

Pitkins & Brooks
Standard Grade
42.00-55.00

Pitkins & Brooks
18.00-21.00

Pitkins & Brooks
Standard Grade
20.00-32.00

Pitkins & Brooks
21.00-24.00

Pitkins & Brooks
12.00-14.00

J. D. Bergen
12.00-18.00

SPOON DISHES and SPOONERS

T. B. Clark & Co.
JEWEL
Empress Spoon
Holder
Each 82.00-92.00

Higgins & Seiter
WHEELER
Spoon Holder
Double Handled
Each 72.00-87.00

Higgins & Seiter
FLORENCE
Spooner, Cut
Each 62.00-82.00

Higgins & Seiter
NAPOLEON
Spooner
Each 82.00-97.0

Averbeck
PRISM
Spooner
Each 72.00-102.00

Averbeck
RUBY
Spooner
Each 77.00-97.00

Averbeck
REGAL
Spooner
Each 112.00-132.00

Higgins & Seiter
WEBSTER
Spooner
Each 92.00-102.00

J. D. Bergen
AVON
Spooner
Each 97.00-127.00

Averbeck
ASHLAND
Spooner
Each 72.00-92.00

Averbeck
SARATOGA
Spooner
Each 62.00-82.00

Pitkins & Brooks
TOOTHPICK HOLDER
2" 18.00-25.0

TOOTHPICK HOLDERS

Pitkins & Brooks
2½" 18.00-24.00

Pitkins & Brooks
TOOTHPICK HOLDER
2½" 17.00-22.00

Pitkins & Brooks
TOOTHPICK HOLDER
2" 15.00-18.00

Pitkins & Brooks
TOOTHPICK HOLDER
2" 17.00-19.0

SPOON DISHES and SPOONERS

Pitkins & Brooks
CORTEZ
P & B Grade
7½'' 62.00-72.00

Pitkins & Brooks
MEADVILLE
Standard Grade
7½'' 42.00-52.00

Pitkins & Brooks
VENICE
P & B Grade
Each 52.00-67.00

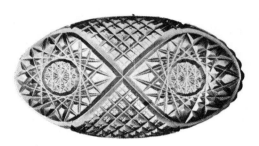

J. D. Bergen
BALTIC
Each 72.00-92.00

Higgins & Seiter
CHRYSANTHEMUM
7¼'' 32.00-47.00

J. D. Bergen
OREGON
Each 32.00-47.00

J. D. Bergen
TAMPA
Each 32.00-47.00

Averbeck
DIAMOND
Each 59.50-89.50

Pitkins & Brooks
RAJAH
P & B Grade
Each 52.00-59.00

T. B. Clark & Co.
MANHATTAN
Each 52.00-67.00

Pitkins & Brooks
CRETE
P & B Grade
6½'' 42.00-62.00

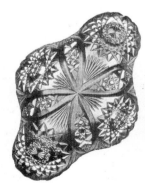

Averbeck
MARIETTA
Each 42.00-62.00

Averbeck
NICE
Each 62.00-77.00

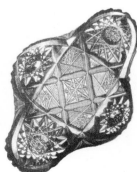

Averbeck
VIENNA
Each 42.00-62.00

SPOON DISHES and SPOONERS

Averbeck
MARIETTA
Each 57.00-67.00

Averbeck
NAPLES
Each 82.00-92.00

Averbeck
DIAMOND
Each 92.00-102.00

Averbeck
VIENNA
Each 47.00-57.00

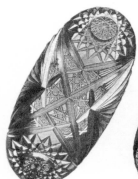

Averbeck
CANTON
Each 47.00-57.00

Averbeck
EMPRESS
Each 57.00-67.00

Averbeck
MARIETTA
Each 57.00-62.00

Averbeck
SARATOGA
Each 57.00-67.00

Averbeck
DIANA
Each 57.00-67.00

Averbeck
SARATOGA
Each 57.00-67.00

Averbeck
DIAMOND
Each 67.00-92.00

Averbeck
CANTON
Each 47.00-57.00

Averbeck
RUBY
Each 42.00-52.00

Averbeck
LIBERTY
Each 47.00-72.00

SPOONS, FORKS and LADLES

Averbeck
VIENNA
Punch Ladle
Each 105.00-120.00

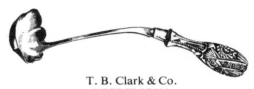

J. D. Bergen
Salad spoon w/Gorham plate,
cut glass handles
Spoon 55.00
Spoon & Fork 90.00-115.00

T. B. Clark & Co.
MANHATTAN
Salad Fork and Spoon
Pair 70.00-85.00

J. D. Bergen
Punch ladle w/Gorham sterling
silver and cut glass handle to
match any pattern
14" 235.00-255.00
16" 355.00-380.00

T. B. Clark & Co.
DESDEMONA
Each 80.00-90.00

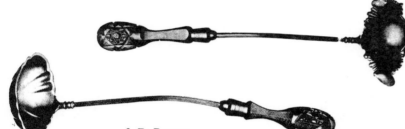

J. D. Bergen
Salad fork, Gorham silver with
cut glass handles
Fork only 80.00
Fork & Spoon 120.00-155.00

Higgins & Seiter
Silver plated w/cut glass handles
Pair 62.00-92.00
Solid silver, gold lined
215.00-265.00

Higgins & Seiter
Silver plated punch ladle, cut
glass handle
Plated .100.00
Solid silver 175.00

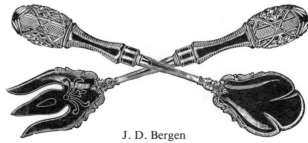

J. D. Bergen
Salad set w/Gorham sterling,
cut glass handle
Pair 305.00-315.00

SYRUP PITCHERS and MUSTARD HOLDERS

J. D. Bergen
PREMIER
Mustard and Plate
Set 80.00-85.00

J. D. Bergen
PREMIER
Mustard
Each 37.00-52.00

J. D. Bergen
MUSTARD
Each 47.00-57.00

J. D. Bergen
OREGON
Half Pt. Syrup
Each 42.00-52.00

Pitkins & Brooks
MUSTARD
Each 27.00-33.00

J. D. Bergen
ELECTRIC
Half Pt. Syrup
Each 50.00-58.00

J. D. Bergen
GLENWOOD
Half Pt. Syrup
Each 60.00-72.00

Pitkins & Brooks
MUSTARD
Each 27.00-33.00

J. D. Bergen
ELECTRIC
Half Pt. Syrup
Each 47.00-63.00

TUMBLERS

T. B. Clark & Co.
19.00-24.00

T. B. Clark & Co.
HENRY VIII
29.00-33.00

J. D. Bergen
GOLF
52.00-57.00

J. D. Bergen
WAVERLY
38.00-44.00

T. B. Clark & Co.
CORAL
41.00-46.00

T. B. Clark & Co.
MANHATTAN
33.00-37.00

Higgins & Seiter
19.00-24.00

Pitkins & Brooks
19.00-24.00

Pitkins & Brooks
WINFIELD
Standard Grade
19.00-27.00

Pitkins & Brooks
19.00-24.00

Pitkins & Brooks
19.00-24.00

Pitkins & Brooks
19.00-24.00

Pitkins & Brooks
MARS
38.50-49.50

Pitkins & Brooks
19.00-24.00

Pitkins & Brooks
Standard Grade
22.00-24.00

Pitkins & Brooks
19.00-24.00

Pitkins & Brooks
19.00-24.00

Pitkins & Brooks
19.00-24.00

STRAWBERRY
DIAMOND FAN
22.00-24.00

J. D. Bergen
ELECTRIC
19.00-24.00

J. D. Bergen
SAVOY
20.00-26.00

Averbeck
MAUD ADAMS
20.00-26.00

Pitkins & Brooks
NELLORE
Standard Grade
20.00-27.00

Higgins & Seiter
FLORENTINE
20.00-27.00

Higgins & Seiter
FLORENTINE
32.00-35.00

TUMBLERS

J. D. Bergen
PREMIER
½ Pt. 33.00-35.00
Champ 31.00-33.00
Whiskey 24.00-26.00

J. D. Bergen
ORIENT
½ Pt. 24.00-26.00
Champ 21.00-24.00
Whiskey 19.00-21.00

J. D. Bergen
GILMORE
½ Pt. 22.00-26.00
Champ 21.00-23.00
Whiskey 19.00-21.00

J. D. Bergen
NEWPORT
½ Pt. 31.00-33.00
Champ 22.00-22.00
Whiskey 22.00-26.00

J. D. Bergen
30.00-32.00

J. D. Bergen
BEDFORD
32.00-35.00

J. D. Bergen
05
26.00-30.00

J. D. Bergen
03
26.00-30.00

J. D. Bergen
07
29.00-31.00

J. D. Bergen
COLONY
30.00-35.00

J. D. Bergen
MARIE
30.00-35.00

J. D. Bergen
DALLAS
41.00-46.00

J. D. Bergen
PROGRESS
41.00-46.00

J. D. Bergen
08
19.00-21.00

T. B. Clark & Co.
WINOLA
21.00-24.00

T. B. Clark & Co.
ARBUTUS
41.00-44.00

T. B. Clark & Co.
JEWEL
32.00-35.00

T. B. Clark & Co.
WINOLA
19.00-21.00

TUMBLERS

Pitkins & Brooks
19.00-21.00

Pitkins & Brooks
19.00-21.00

Pitkins & Brooks
Standard Grade
19.00-21.00

Pitkins & Brooks
Standard Grade
24.00-26.00

Pitkins & Brooks
19.00-21.00

Pitkins & Brooks
Standard Grade
21.00-23.00

J. D. Bergen
ARLINGTON
14.00-26.00

J. D. Bergen
EVANS
24.00-26.00

J. D. Bergen
U.S.
19.00-21.00

J. D. Bergen
GOLDENROD
30.00-33.00

J. D. Bergen
NEWPORT
19.00-21.00

J. D. Bergen
RESERVE
15.00-19.00

J. D. Bergen
GOLF
15.00-22.00

J. D. Bergen
ATLAS
15.00-19.00

J. D. Bergen
ROLAND
19.00-21.00

J. D. Bergen
BALTIMORE
21.00-23.00

J. D. Bergen
ANSONIA
33.00-35.00

J. D. Bergen
ETHEL
33.00-35.00

J. D. Bergen
03
13.00-20.00

J. D. Bergen
KNOX
13.00-20.00

Pitkins & Brooks
13.00-20.00

Pitkins & Brooks
13.00-20.00

Higgins & Seiter
CUT STAR
33.00-35.00

Higgins & Seiter
NAPOLEON
33.00-35.00

T. B. Clark & Co.
WINOLA
19.00-23.00

137

TUMBLERS

Averbeck
NICE
41.00-46.00

Averbeck
SARATOGA
30.00-32.00

Averbeck
ALABAMA
21.00-23.00

Averbeck
RADIUM
30.00-32.00

Averbeck
DAYTON
21.00-23.00

Averbeck
BOSTON
30.00-32.00

Averbeck
GENOA
32.00-35.00

Averbeck
RUBY
26.00-33.00

Averbeck
TRIXY
21.00-23.00

Averbeck
ACME
52.00-71.00

Averbeck
FLORIDA
19.00-21.00

Averbeck
MAUD ADAMS
19.00-21.00

Averbeck
LIBERTY
33.00-37.00

Averbeck
RUBY
33.00-37.00

Averbeck
MAINE
33.00-37.00

Averbeck
MAUD ADAMS
21.00-23.00

Averbeck
VIENNA
26.00-33.00

Averbeck
MELBA
19.00-21.00

Averbeck
GEORGIA
21.00-24.00

Averbeck
GENOA
30.00-32.00

Averbeck
LIBERTY
26.50-28.50

Averbeck
TRIXY
19.00-21.00

Averbeck
GENOA
26.50-28.50

Averbeck
VIENNA
22.00-26.50

Averbeck
MELBA
19.00-22.00

Averbeck
FLORIDA
22.00-29.00

Averbeck
LIBERTY
27.50-30.00

VASES

Pitkins & Brooks
P & B Grade
10" 89.00-99.00
12" 105.00-115.00
14" 136.00-152.00

J. D. Bergen
TROPHY
6" 63.00-73.00
8" 73.00-84.00
10" 84.00-94.00
12" 94.00-110.00
14" 110.00-131.00

J. D. Bergen
DIXON
8" 105.00-120.00
10" 136.00-162.00
12" 189.00-215.00
14" 215.00-257.00

Averbeck
NICE
12" 252.00-262.00
15" 273.00-294.00
18" 325.00-388.00

Averbeck
RADIUM
8" 70.00-81.00
10" 76.00-86.00
12" 97.00-107.00
14" 118.00-113.00

Averbeck
LIBERTY
8" 89.00-99.00
10" 99.00-110.00
12" 126.00-136.00
14" 136.00-152.00

Averbeck
NAPLES
17" 346.00-399.00

Averbeck
SARATOGA
14" 288.00-367.00

139

VASES

J. D. Bergen
SUNBEAM
Two Pieces
21" 525.00-630.00

Pitkins & Brooks
STAR
Vase
P & B Grade
10" 187.00-208.00
13" 220.00-252.00
16" 273.00-315.00

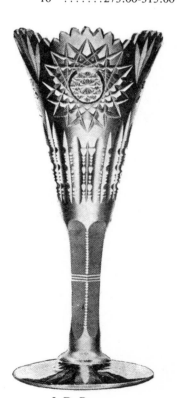

J. D. Bergen
RUTLAND
6" 52.00-73.00
8" 73.00-94.00
10" 94.00-105.00
12" 105.00-131.00
14" 136.00-157.00

VASES

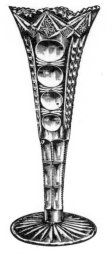

Higgins & Seiter
FLORENTINE
8" 52.00-63.00
10" 73.00-84.00
12" 84.00-94.00
14" 94.00-105.00
16" 131.00-157.00

Pitkins & Brooks
8" 68.00-80.00
9" 78.00-91.00
10" 89.00-105.00
12" 99.00-131.00

Averbeck
DAISY
8" 89.00-115.00
10" 115.00-126.00
12" 126.00-168.00
14" 168.00-220.00

Higgins & Seiter
EVERETT
8" 52.00-73.00
10" 73.00-84.00
12" 84.00-110.00
14" 115.00-136.00
16" 136.00-168.00

Higgins & Seiter
INDIA
12" 157.00-168.00

T. B. Clark & Co.
PALMETTO
7" 57.00-73.00
8" 99.00-105.00
10" 110.00-126.00
12" 131.00-147.00
15" 173.00-210.00
18" 231.00-273.00

VASES

T. B. Clark & Co.
HEROIC
Each 73.00-84.00

T. B. Clark & Co.
ORIENT
9" 136.00-157.00
12" 168.00-189.00

T. B. Clark & Co.
PALMETTO
Large 136.00-168.00
Small 115.00-136.00

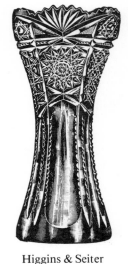

Higgins & Seiter
B 9/602
9" 73.00-84.00
10" 84.00-99.00
12" 105.00-136.00

Higgins & Seiter
FLORENTINE
8" 84.00-105.00
10" 105.00-126.00
12" 136.00-157.00

T. B. Clark & Co.
ADONIS
15" 199.00-236.00
18" 236.00-283.00

Pitkins & Brooks
P & B Grade
12½" 189.00-220.00

Averbeck
ALABAMA
6" 47.00-57.00
8" 57.00-73.00
10" 78.00-105.00
12" 115.00-125.00
14" 131.00-156.00

Averbeck
PRISM
8" 84.00-94.00

T. B. Clark & Co.
HENRY VIII
7" 63.00-73.00
8" 84.00-89.00
10" 89.00-105.00
12" 105.00-136.00
15" 136.00-157.00

Pitkins & Brooks
BELMONT BUD
P & B Grade
Each 78.00

Higgins & Seiter
NAPEOLEON
4½" 57.00

VASES

Pitkins & Brooks
ROSABELLA
Standard Grade
8'' 94.00-105.00
10'' 99.00-131.00
12'' 136.00-183.00

Averbeck
ASHLAND
6'' 52.00-63.00
8'' 78.00-89.00
10'' 89.00-105.00
12'' 105.00-131.00
14'' 131.00-157.00

Pitkins & Brooks
Each 42.00-63.00

Pitkins & Brooks
P & B Grade
10½'' 131.00-168.00

Pitkins & Brooks
HIAWATHA SWEET
PEA
P & B Grade
8'' 126.00-157.00

Pitkins & Brooks
ARANS
P & B Grade
10'' 168.00-189.00
12'' 194.00-215.00
14'' 215.00-252.00

Pitkins & Brooks
TECK VASE
P & B Grade
10'' 115.00-131.00
12'' 141.00-168.00

Pitkins & Brooks
ARANS
P & B Grade
14'' 210.00-236.00

Pitkins & Brooks
EYES
P & B Grade
12'' 115.00-141.00

Averbeck
DIAMOND
12'' 210.00-240.00

Averbeck
RUBY
Each 147.00-178.00

T. B. Clark & Co.
HENRI VIII
7'' 89.00-99.00
9'' 94.00-126.00
12'' 126.00-147.00

Averbeck
FLORIDA
6'' 36.00-47.00
8'' 47.00-57.00
10'' 63.00-73.00
12'' 78.00-99.00
14'' 99.00-115.00

VASES

J. D. Bergen
NEVADA
8'' 183.00-204.00
10'' 220.00-262.00
12'' 262.00-273.00

J. D. Bergen
FAUST
6'' 99.00-115.00
7'' 126.00-147.00
8'' 141.00-157.00
9'' 183.00-220.00

Pitkins & Brooks
AURORA BOREALIS
P & B Grade
6½'' 136.00-157.00

Averbeck
ASHLAND
5'' 52.00-63.00

Averbeck
LIBERTY
Each 63.00-78.00

T. B. Clark & Co.
WINOLA
Each 52.00-63.00

T. B. Clark & Co.
DESDEMONA
Each . .231.00-294.00

T. B. Clark & Co.
4'' 57.00-73.00
6'' 78.00-99.00

Averbeck
MELBA
4'' 52.00-68.00

Averbeck
ASHLAND
4'' 42.00-63.00

J. D. Bergen
ELECTRIC
3-Handled Rose Ball
3½'' 42.00-63.00

T. B. Clark & Co.
MANHATTAN
6'' 115.00-131.00
7'' 147.00-162.00
8'' 152.00-183.00

Averbeck
FLORIDA
5'' 73.00-84.00
6'' 94.00-105.00
7'' 120.00-136.00

J. D. Bergen
PREMIER
3½'' 50.00-55.00
4½'' 55.00-65.00
6'' 80.00-90.00
7'' 90.00-100.00
8'' 110.00-125.00
9'' 150.00-185.00

Pitkins & Brooks
VIOLET BUD VASE
P & B Grade
5'' 63.00-78.00

VASES

J. D. Bergen
GOLDENROD
3'' 52.00-63.00
4'' 63.00-73.00
5'' 73.00-84.00
6'' 94.00-136.00

J. D. Bergen
CLIFTON
9'' 210.00-220.00
12'' 220.00-241.00
15'' 283.00-304.00

J. D. Bergen
NEVADA
3'' 52.00-68.00
4'' 63.00-78.00
6'' 84.00-99.00

Averbeck
GENOA
10'' 245.00-268.00

Averbeck
PRISCILLA
Each 52.00-79.00

Averbeck
GENOA
2-Handled
12'' 315.00-367.00

J. D. Bergen
GOLDENROD
7'' 157.50-189.50
8'' 199.50-241.50
10'' 241.50-262.50
12'' 283.50-325.50

Pitkins & Brooks
AMANDA
P & B Grade
10'' 131.00-165.00
12'' 170.00-196.00
14'' 196.00-220.00

Pitkins & Brooks
GLEE VASE
P & B Grade
8'' 94.00-131.00

VASES

Averbeck
MELBA
6" 52.00-68.00
8" 63.00-79.00
10" 73.00-89.00
12" 84.00-100.00
14" 105.00-136.00

J. D. Bergen
UNITY
9" 241.00-278.00
12" 278.00-310.00
15" 315.00-341.00

J. D. Bergen
SHELDON
8" 105.00-115.00
10" 147.00-168.00
12" 189.00-220.00
14" 220.00-252.00

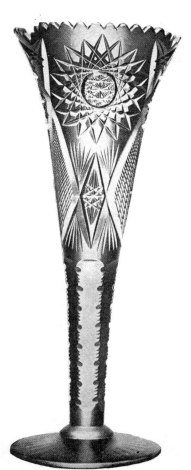

Pitkins & Brooks
ROSE VASE
P & B Grade
8" 160.00-175.00

Averbeck
VIENNA
8" 154.00-186.00
10" 181.00-205.00
12" 226.00-270.00

J. D. Bergen
CLEVELAND
6" 51.00-68.00
8" 68.00-73.00
10" 79.00-105.00
12" 105.00-131.00
14" 110.00-147.00

Pitkins & Brooks
BERRIE FLOWER
HOLDER
P & B Grade
8" 184.00-236.00

VASES

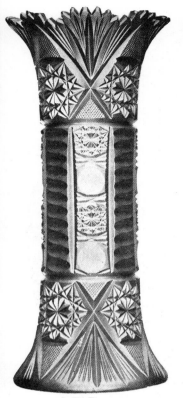

J. D. Bergen
LAMONT

8" 121.00-136.00
10" 136.00-157.00
12" 163.00-178.00
14" 163.00-189.00
16" 205.00-231.00

J. D. Bergen
EGYPTIAN

9" 136.00-178.00
12" 184.00-231.00
15" 199.00-241.00

J. D. Bergen
GOLDENROD

8" 142.00-152.00
10" 152.00-163.00
12" 163.00-173.00

J. D. Bergen
BANGOR

8" 58.00-73.00
10" 68.00-84.00
12" 79.00-94.00
14" 100.00-115.00

J. D. Bergen
BELMORE

6" 79.00-89.00
8" 100.00-115.00
10" 121.00-136.00
12" 152.00-189.00
14" 163.00-199.00

J. D. Bergen
CHELSEA

6" 58.00-73.00
7" 79.00-84.00
8" 84.00-94.00
10" 94.00-105.00
12" 105.00-115.00

J. D. Bergen
RUTLAND

6" 58.00-73.00
8" 79.00-84.00
10" 84.00-94.00
12" 94.00-105.00
14" 105.00-115.00

Pitkins & Brooks
TAMPA
P & B Grade

12" 163.00-205.00

VASES

Pitkins & Brooks
P & B Grade
10" 115.00-142.00

J. D. Bergen
COLONY
9" 174.00-194.00
12" 205.00-231.00

J. D. Bergen
KENWOOD
12" 205.00-226.00
15" 231.00-262.00
18" 241.00-273.00

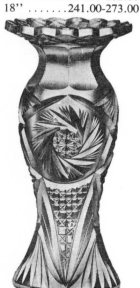

Averbeck
ROME
11" 157.50-178.50

J. D. Bergen
CALUMET
9" 142.00-157.00
12" 157.00-189.00
15" 178.00-220.00

Pitkins & Brooks
TOKA
P & B Grade
10" 121.00-136.00
12" 136.00-157.00
15" 152.00-210.00

Pitkins & Brooks
CHRISTIANA VASE
Standard Grade
8" 100.00-110.00
10" 110.00-126.00
12" 121.00-136.00
14" 142.00-189.00

148

VASES

Pitkins & Brooks
Each 58.00-89.00

Pitkins & Brooks
DIAMOND
P & B Grade
11" 152.00-194.00

Pitkins & Brooks
P & B Grade
8" 105.00-115.00
10" 115.00-136.00
13" 136.00-147.00
15" 152.00-168.00
18" 168.00-199.00
20" 292.00-241.00

Pitkins & Brooks
FORGET-ME-NOT
Vase, Engraved
P & B Grade
2" 273.00-325.00

Pitkins & Brooks
TRUSELLA VASE
P & B Grade
10" 205.00-231.00

Pitkins & Brooks
ELECTRA VASE
P & B Grade
10" 231.00-241.00
12" 236.00-252.00
14" 236.00-262.00
16" 289.00-325.00

Pitkins & Brooks
BERRIE
P & B Grade
14" 220.50-241.50
18" 283.50-325.50

Pitkins & Brooks
WALDORF
P & B Grade
10" 184.00-194.00
12" 199.00-210.00
14" 215.00-236.00
16" 262.00-299.00
18" 325.00-378.00

Pitkins & Brooks
TECK VASE
P & B Grade
9½" 184.00-194.00

Pitkins & Brooks
ORLEANS VASE
P & B Grade
11" 121.00-142.00

Pitkins & Brooks
WALDORF
P & B Grade
8½" 157.00-184.00

VASES

J. D. Bergen
RIALTO

12" 304.00-331.00
14" 336.00-373.00

J. D. Bergen
QUEEN

10" 163.00-184.00
12" 189.00-205.00
14" 210.00-247.00

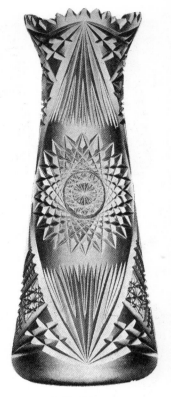

J. D. Bergen
LYDA

9" 150.00-215.00
12" 126.00-199.00
15" 194.00-236.00

J. D. Bergen
UTAH

4" 73.00-94.00
6" 150.00-126.00
8" 126.00-163.00

J. D. Bergen
NUTWOOD

4" 73.00-94.00
6" 89.00-150.00
8" 126.00-152.00

J. D. Bergen
CORA

6" 58.00-63.00
8" 63.00-73.00
10" 68.00-79.00
12" 84.00-89.00
14" 115.00-126.00

VASES

J. D. Bergen
NUTWOOD

8"	189.00-220.00
10"	205.00-236.00
12"	220.00-262.00

J. D. Bergen
WALLACE

8"	220.00-241.00
10"	236.00-252.00
12"	268.00-299.00

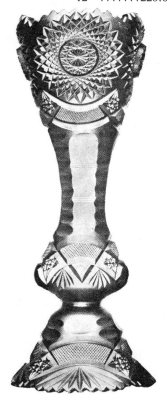

J. D. Bergen
PYRAMID

9"	152.00-163.00
12"	168.00-220.00
15"	216.00-262.00

Pitkins & Brooks
COLUMBIA
Standard Grade

8"	56.00-73.00
10"	79.00-84.00
12"	89.00-94.00
14"	100.00-126.00

Pitkins & Brooks
Standard Grade

8"	57.00-73.00
10"	79.00-84.00
12"	89.00-94.00
14"	100.00-126.00

Averbeck
GENOA

10"	163.00-178.00
12"	184.00-194.00
14"	231.00-262.00

WATER SETS

J. D. Bergen
NEWPORT
Set 185.00-225.00

J. D. Bergen
BEDFORD
Set 142.00-184.00

J. D. Bergen
BOSTON/ATLAS
Set 94.00-126.00

J. D. Bergen
PREMIER
Set 225.00-257.00

J. D. Bergen
ANSONIA
Set 200.00-240.00

J. D. Bergen
GOLF
Set 157.00-168.00

WATER SETS

Pitkins & Brooks
METROPOLE
8-Piece Water Set
Set 105.00-131.00

Pitkins & Brooks
Standard Grade
8-Piece Water Set
Set 94.00-122.00

Pitkins & Brooks
CARRIE
8-Piece Water Set
Set 150.00-185.00

Pitkins & Brooks
CARLTON
8-Piece Water Set
Set 94.00-147.00

Pitkins & Brooks
RUTH
8-Piece Water Set
Set 150.00-200.00

WATER SETS

Pitkins & Brooks
CARNATION
8-Piece Water Set
Set 157.00-210.00

Pitkins & Brooks
BERMUDA
8-Piece Water Set
Set 236.00-262.00

J. D. Bergen
GOLF
Set 157.00-173.00

INDEX

INDEX